BALANCE FOR SENIORS

50, 60 and Beyond

Live Without Fear of Falling

Improve Stability, Posture and Boost Confidence

30 chair and 20 bodyweight illustrated exercises + 50 videos

DAVID O'CONNOR

BALANCE EXERCISE

FOR SENIORS 50, 60 AND BEYOND

Your Guide to Banish the Fear of Falling.

Fully illustrated, video supported, home exercises to improve Balance, Posture and boost Self-Confidence.

- **30** Chair Exercises
- **20** Bodyweight Exercises
- **8** Week Workout Plans (low, medium and high mobility)
- **50** Videos to aid correct performance to maximise benefits.

Never Fear Falling Again!

FREE BONUS FITNESS MATERIAL TO HELP YOU ACHIEVE YOUR GOAL

To ensure you gain as much value as possible from Balance Exercise For Seniors 50, 60 and Beyond, I've put together some additional free bonus materials to help you achieve your goals, including:

- **60 Day Beginners Workout Plan** provided as printable PDF documents
- **4 Fitness Word Puzzles**. As a bit of fun to help maintain brain fitness too.
- **Direct access to the exercise videos** from our members area (without scanning QR Codes)

- **Members Only Access** to videos showing the exercises contained in each of the workout plans (not available via QR codes from within the book)
- **Monthly Newsletter** on topics to help you succeed on your fitness journey.

GET YOUR FREE BONUS MATERIAL

TABLE OF CONTENTS

FORWARD

It is important to recognize that seniors, like any other demographic, have varying degrees of mobility and a one size fits all approach to balance exercises simply does not work. Therefore, exercises and workouts within this book are designated as low, medium and high mobility. We provide two methods to determine which category best meets your current needs, Timed Up & Go (TUG) and One-Legged Stance Test (OLST). We encourage you take one or both tests and then to follow the appropriate exercises and workouts.

As your mobility improves consider incorporate exercises from the next mobility group.

INTRODUCTION

By 2050, the percentage of people over 60 will rise from 12 to 22% globally, and 35% of those people will suffer from mobility issues [1]. A loss in mobility can affect many aspects of your lifestyle. For example, it can increase your daily expenditure (e.g. paying for cabs to transport you places), limit your independence, and affect your physical and mental health.

There is a commonly held belief that the reduction in mobility as you age is unavoidable and that once this begins, you cannot reverse it. While it is undoubtedly true that prevention is easier than cure, it is untrue that there is nothing that can be done to address this issue.

So, how can balance exercises help? Improving your balance is about maintaining your equilibrium and building strength, mobility, and flexibility. You are strengthening your core muscles, legs, arms, back, shoulders, and chest.

Improving your balance through exercise will help reduce your fall risk, making you less likely to suffer from injury. Improved balance can also help you lead a more active lifestyle. There will be more sports available for you to participate in. You will be able to be more competitive, run faster, throw further, and jump higher.

If all of this sounds too difficult for you, then learning how to perform balance exercises is more crucial to you than ever before. Don't get held back by limiting beliefs or conventional wisdom. You may not be slam dunking any time soon, but no matter how immobile you are, you can improve your situation via exercise.

This book provides you with all the tools you need to improve your balance, coordination, strength, power, and fitness. Each exercise is labelled as either low mobility, medium mobility, or high mobility. So if you have limited mobility, you still have an extensive range of exercises you can participate in.

One of the limitations of exercise books such as this is that they cannot train every person individually. This book does not know your medical history, it does not know what injuries you have or mobility issues you have suffered from.

But that does not mean that the book cannot help you. Always talk to your physician before carrying out a new training program. If your physician recommends hiring a personal trainer or physio, this book can be combined with that.

Suppose you already know how to exercise around your mobility issues. In that case, this book is an excellent tool for increasing variety in your workouts and improving other aspects of your fitness and coordination.

How to Use This Book

This book aims to get you to perform regular workouts that can improve balance and other benefits associated with exercise.

It teaches you many exercises, including using a chair, a set of light dumbbells, resistance bands, or your body weight. Many exercises will have progressions and regressions to suit differing fitness and mobility levels.

Each exercise will have a thorough description so that you know exactly how to perform it safely and competently. You will also know what equipment is required for each exercise and any safety tips you may need.

The book then provides you with several different workouts. Each workout is designed for people with varying levels of mobility. If you have limited mobility, you can follow a workout that suits your capabilities.

If you are highly mobile and have no injuries or limitations, you can follow a more intensive workout that will challenge you much more.

What is a Realistic Outcome from This Book?

According to the Centers for Disease Control and Prevention (CDC), seniors require a minimum of 150 minutes of exercise each week [2]. The CDC also recommends performing strength-based exercises twice each week.

According to a 2013 study, less than half of adults aged 65-74 achieve this target, dropping to around 33% for people over 75 [3]. This is the context in which this book is written.

Most seniors are not exercising enough to meet the minimum requirements for health and vitality. As you age, this inevitably leads to a significant loss of balance, coordination, strength, and cardiovascular fitness.

No exercise program can lessen the effects of ageing. As we age, our hormone production will change, our bones will become less dense, and our muscles will lose size and strength. This can all lead to an increased risk of falls and then injury.

But, regular exercise, particularly exercises that can improve balance and coordination, can help to slow down or even stop the decline. If you follow the program long enough, you can see improvements from your younger days!

Following the exercises and workouts in this book will help you:

- Improve your balance
- Reduce your risk of falling
- Increase your mobility
- Improve your confidence and self-assuredness
- Increase your strength and fitness
- Protect your independence as you age

These are just some of the benefits available, but the last benefit is perhaps the most important. Many people with balance issues find that they can become isolated as they age. For example, being unable to walk places or even drive your car can reduce the size of the area you travel in.

Unless this issue is addressed, it will only get worse. Luckily, you can improve your balance with some of the most simple exercises around. For example, changing how you sit on a chair can help you build coordination and strength in your legs and core.

Once you have mastered the simplest movements, this book can help you to move on to more complex and challenging variations. For example, you can progress from sitting on a chair to sitting on a chair with one leg raised in front of you. One of the toughest tests of balance for people of any age.

But all this is possible with practice and commitment. Picking up this book and opening it demonstrates your commitment to mastering balance and coordination. So let's move on to the next step in your journey.

Meet the Author

Who am I? Well, I'm a Personal Trainer and proud to say I've been studying and practicing physical training for most of my life and can appreciate the benefits this conditioning has done for my own health, not to mention many others whom I have trained so they were able to benefit from this same training and health information. Following are a few notes and quotes to give you a quick overview of my background and experiences, so I can let you know how to start, improve, and finally become an expert in order to achieve a better quality of life, benefiting from my knowledge, and this new exercise method, the benefits of which numerous academic studies have verified, that continues to grow in popularity.

- A fitness nut since my days at UCLA, cross-fit, trail running, and skiing are still my passions. During the last 25 years as a Ski Instructor and Personal Trainer, I've trained people of all ages and abilities to achieve their fitness goals. A couple of years ago my father required assistance to improve his health, having become increasingly sedentary with each passing year. It took a sustained effort to get him to accept that it's never too late to get fit, certainly not at just 65 years of age!
- I guided my father through a simple yet progressively challenging home exercise program, and introduced him to healthier eating habits appropriate for his stage of life and individual body type, also taking into account his specific needs due to a medical condition. Today, he lives a fulfilling, active Californian lifestyle, regularly beating me on the golf course.
- Another source of inspiration for me is George Jedenoff. He's the oldest living graduate of Stanford Graduate School of Business (GSB) and was still skiing Snowbird at the age of 103. George attributes a daily exercise program and a positive mindset for this vitality, "***That's why I'm still here because I've been adaptable and optimistic all my life".*** If you get a moment,

watch George's video it is inspirational. He celebrated his 105th birthday in July 2023, and hopes to get at least a couple of days skiing this season at a lower altitude resort than Snowbird. The QR code below links to George's video where he shows his daily workout routine. Please take a look, I'm sure you will find it inspirational!

SCAN FOR VIDEO

- Through extensive research, teaching many different forms of exercise over my 25-year coaching career, and working with trainers and specialists both in the USA and Europe, I've become an authority on the latest workouts and lifestyle habits that will allow anyone, especially seniors, to learn and adopt effective, efficient, and safe fitness routines. The Balance Exercises and Workouts contained here will provide positive results.

- The mobility level required for each exercise is specified and workout plans are provided for Low, Medium, and High Mobility.

What sets this book and the other books in the *For Seniors 50, 60 and Beyond* series apart is that I use my expertise and experience to describe each exercise in detail, so you can easily understand and follow along at your own pace. I keep the descriptions simple, but I still carefully explain the movements and positions with sufficient detail so you can perform each exercise correctly and avoid injury.

Often, no matter how precise a book's exercise instructions or detailed the accompanying illustrations are, they may still leave you unsure how to perform it. Incorrectly performed exercises reduce their effectiveness and can lead to injury, a possibility that increases with age. That is why I want you to be able to see how to perform each exercise to remove all ambiguity. Therefore, each exercise in this book is not only illustrated but accompanied by a QR Code, scan it on your mobile to watch a video clip of the exercise being performed.

My goal is to write fitness books that help you get fit and lead a healthy life, the best life possible!

I'm excited to share my knowledge with you now, and help you improve your quality of life.

Leave a Review:

If you enjoy this book and it helps you achieve your goals, as I most definitely trust it will, please take a minute to leave a short Amazon review. Your feedback will help others considering starting their fitness journey.

SCAN TO LEAVE AMAZON REVIEW

Let's get started with Chapter 1!

CHAPTER 1

How to Prevent Injury and Increase Independence as You Age

"Knowing how to grow old is the master work of wisdom"

Henri Frederic Amiel

In your 20s, falling over is seen as funny. The term pratfall was coined due to the hilarity that falling over can invoke in others. Of course, this does not apply to all falls, but most falls in young people are unlikely to cause injury, and once that person has climbed back up again, it can become a humorous anecdote.

Falling over in your 60s is not funny. It can be pretty dangerous. According to the CDC, 36 million falls per year in the US involve seniors [4], resulting in 32,000 deaths and 3 million trips to the emergency department. In addition, 20% of falls in seniors will result in broken bones or head injuries.

Any fall resulting in broken bones will affect you for a long time. Many seniors who break their bones can expect to suffer from mobility issues for the remainder of their lives.

There are, of course, many options for seniors once they have fallen. Surgery, physiotherapy, a bag of frozen peas (depending on the severity of the fall), pain medication, and changes to their lifestyle. But it is fair to say that prevention is better than a cure.

If your balance is good, your coordination is optimal, and you have strong, flexible muscles, your chances of falling over are significantly reduced. In addition, if you do fall over, you are less likely to be seriously injured, and your recovery will be faster. Your body will also be able to adjust to mobility issues more efficiently.

Rehab vs Prehab

Rehabilitation can be a long and challenging process, and it is used to help you to return to full fitness and mobility after an accident or injury. Depending on the severity, this process may last a few weeks or years. Some forms of rehab can last a lifetime, though this is rare.

Prehab is a term for training (balance, coordination, strength, flexibility etc.) to help reduce the risk of getting injured in the first place. Of course, you cannot guarantee that you won't be injured, but you can lower your odds.

A misconception is that prehab exercises are similar to rehabilitation exercises, but they are not. When performing rehab, you often have to adjust to your injury and lack mobility, so the workouts are customised.

With prehab, you are performing regular exercises that can improve your balance as well as other aspects of fitness. The exercises are designed to test your balance and improve it gradually. So even if you already have mobility issues, you can prehab to prevent further problems.

People with poor mobility in their legs are far more likely to injure themselves than those without, so prehab is more critical. Sadly, when it comes to injuries, lightning can strike twice or more.

Ten Benefits of Regular Balance Exercises for Seniors

Balance exercises work best when they are performed regularly for a substantial time. It's no use performing ten reps once per month and giving up after your second session. You need to train often and be constantly looking to improve on your previous best.

If you can follow your balance exercise training program regularly for at least eight weeks, you can expect to see the following benefits.

1. **Increased Strength -** Strength and balance have more in common than you might think and are both inextricably linked. Without strength in your muscles, your balance will suffer, and without balance and coordination, it can be hard to build and maintain strength.

   Training regularly for balance will help to build strength in your muscles. It can help to increase power, but also muscular endurance. Allowing you to hold your balance for longer, something that can be very important as you age.

   Building strength may not be your goal when picking this book up, but it should be. Increasing the strength of your muscles and bones can help to prevent frailty and injury. It can improve your independence, and it can improve your body composition.

   The more muscle you have, the higher your metabolic rate and the lower your body fat percentage.

2. **Increased Mobility -** Mobility and flexibility are often confused or conflated. The definition of mobility is being able to move freely and unimpeded. You can be flexible without being mobile, and you can be mobile without being particularly flexible.

   Performing regular balancing exercises can make a massive difference to your mobility. This is because balance exercises strengthen the muscles required to be fully mobile. Balance exercises can also reduce your risk of injury, improve your coordination, and help you to move around more freely.

   The benefits of having improved mobility are endless. Poor mobility can prevent you from playing your favourite sports, performing household tasks, or even leaving your house. As you age, your mobility will become more and more important to you.

3. **Reduced Injury Risk -** Reducing your risk of injury is highly beneficial. Older people are much more likely to have their lives affected by even a minor injury. Balance exercises can minimise injury risk in several ways.

Firstly, they increase your mobility and core strength, making you more manoeuvrable and agile. This means you can traverse rough terrain or walk home from the shops without stumbling or tripping yourself up.

The increased mobility and agility can also help you maintain your balance when you trip or fall, so you can get yourself back upright and avoid hitting the floor.

Your body will also be more durable and able to withstand the shock of falling over when the worst happens. Stronger and denser bones can survive a fall better, and muscles can survive by being more flexible.

Preventing injury, or mitigating the effects of an injury, is something that all older people should prioritise as they age.

4. **Improved Coordination -** Balance exercises can help you to improve your coordination. This is important because coordination skills can reduce as we age. A lack of coordination can lead to increased injury risk and chronic injuries due to poor form during repetitive tasks such as walking.

Good coordination means you can play sports and lead a more active life. This can help to improve your physical, mental, and cognitive health.

5. **Protects Your Independence -** Protecting your independence is such an underrated benefit of any form of exercise. As we age, our bodies find specific tasks much more complex than they did previously. This can be down to coordination, balance, core strength, injuries, or illness.

   It can affect how you live your life. For example, let's say you have limited shoulder mobility. This can stop you from driving your car safely, reaching for items on high shelves, or carrying heavy bags.

   These issues would make a trip to the shops almost impossible! You would need to get someone to either give you a lift to the shops or do your shopping for you. This is not only inconvenient, but it can take away life's little luxuries.

   Shopping can feel like a chore, but it is also an opportunity to hunt for bargains, purchase gifts for friends, or grab an impulsive item.

   Regular balancing exercises can help improve your mobility and slow down age-related decline. This can help you to stay independent for longer (possibly indefinitely) and enjoy life to the fullest.

6. **Increased Cognition -** The connection between exercise and cognition is well established. For example, a 2009 study found a clear relationship between regular physical activity and improved attention, speed of thought, and memory, and it appears to reduce the risk of developing Alzheimer's disease [5].

   This applies to all forms of exercise, from cardio to weight lifting, and yes, it even includes balance exercises. It does this by altering brain structure, for example, increasing blood flow to the brain and improving brain cell health. According to Harvard Health Publishing, it can also help reduce insulin resistance and inflammation, which can harm cognition over time [6].

   Regular exercise can also help to improve your mental health (see below) and your sleep quality, which can positively affect your cognition.

   As we age, our cognition can begin to decline, and the correlation between people who have less independence, perform less exercise, and have poor cognition is known to science.

   Many seniors are understandably anxious to preserve their cognition and often spend time improving their brain power with brain teasers, books, puzzles, and similar thought-provoking activities.

But the science seems to support the idea that you would be better placed to protect your cognition by exercising regularly. Particularly if that exercise can help you increase your independence, boost your mood, and sleep better.

Combining brain training and exercise is probably your best bet for supporting and protecting your cognition. Or even boosting it.

7. **Improved Mood -** Most people know that cognition can suffer as we age, but the effect of age on mood and mental health is less established. There is a lot of evidence that exercising regularly can help to improve your mood, reducing depression, anxiety, and stress [7].

   Your mood can be negatively affected by many factors. These can affect you at any age; it's not just seniors! For example, poor sleep quality can lead to increased cortisol production, lowered testosterone in men, and increased stress.

   Another cause of low mood is increased body fat, which can disrupt healthy hormone production and cause inflammation. Increased body fat can also cause bad sleep quality and contributes to sleep apnea.

One of the perceived benefits of retiring from work is the loss of stress, but the truth is that work is not the only cause of stress. Family, economics, world news, and your health can all lead to increased stress, which can, in turn, affect mood.

Exercise cannot cure all causes of low mood, but it can help. Regular exercise can help both directly and indirectly. It can directly improve mood by increasing blood flow to the brain (as we saw with cognition) and can affect the limbic system. Enhancing mood and motivation [8].

It can indirectly affect mood by improving sleep, reducing body fat, increasing independence and socialisation, and regulating hormone production.

8. **Appetite Regulation -** The effect of exercise on appetite is fascinating. Many people worry about overeating, thanks to a large appetite. But as we age, the opposite can also be true. Seniors can often report losing their appetite.

   Exercise does not necessarily cause you to eat more or less food. Instead, it regulates hunger and satiety, which can help keep your appetite in check. If you are currently under eating because your appetite has dropped, then regular exercise can help to fix this.

Suppose you are currently overeating, often due to stress, poor sleep, depression, or excess body fat (which can affect hormones). In that case, regular exercise can help with these and lead to a reduced appetite.

Regular exercise can help you to control your appetite for positive results. It should be noted that many factors can positively and negatively affect appetite, and training can't solve them all. But for many people, embarking on a new regular exercise program may lead to positive improvements [9].

9. **Weight Management -** As with appetite regulation, many seniors struggle to manage weight as they age. Whether losing weight or gaining weight, it can be hard to maintain a healthy weight without regular exercise.

   If you have read the previous eight benefits, then you will know that there are many ways in which regular exercise can help to influence your body fat and muscle levels. The most obvious is that exercise can raise your metabolic rate and burn calories.

But it can also increase muscle mass, improve sleep quality, help balance your hormones, improve your mood, and regulate your appetite. All these can help you reach and maintain a healthy weight.

10. **Improved Sleep Quality -** The final benefit on this list is improved sleep quality. As we age, our suprachiasmatic nucleus (SCN) begins to deteriorate. This affects circadian rhythms, which you may remember control when you feel tired, energetic, or hungry [10].

    Hormonal changes can also affect sleep quality, as can some of the lifestyle factors discussed in this chapter: mood, cognition, appetite, body fat, and activity level.

    All of these lifestyle factors affect sleep, and in turn, sleep can exacerbate the lifestyle factors. They are creating a vicious circle. Most health professionals believe that sleep, diet, and exercise are all tied together and that proper health requires all three to be optimal.

    Luckily, a lot of evidence supports the claim that regular exercise can improve sleep quality. For example, a 2010 Journal of Sleep Medicine study found that aerobic exercise can improve self-reported sleep quality in older adults with insomnia [11].

The study concluded that:

"Aerobic physical activity with sleep hygiene education is an effective treatment approach to improve sleep quality, mood and quality of life in older adults with chronic insomnia."

It also found that regular aerobic exercise could help to reduce depressive symptoms, one of the leading causes of poor sleep quality in adults.

Why Balance Exercises, in Particular, Are Crucial for Independence in Seniors

Balance is a great term and one that we will use in this book, but the correct scientific term is postural stability. It describes your ability to maintain your centre of gravity. There are two forms of postural stability; static and dynamic.

"An example of static postural stability is standing quietly without movement, while dynamic postural stability refers to the ability to maintain posture while performing specific movements, such as reaching forward or walking." Rogers, Page, Takeshima 2013 [12]

As you age, your body will begin to lose postural stability (balance), partly due to your body's natural ageing process and partly due to changes in circumstances.

If you don't test your balance often, your body's ability to balance will suffer. In the same way that if you stopped practising the piano for 30 years, you would be pretty rusty when picking it up again.

CHAPTER 2

What to Know Before You Start Your First Workout

"Your present circumstances don't determine where you can go; they merely determine where you start."

Nido Qubein

Starting a new exercise routine can be a thoroughly exciting experience, and many people find that they are highly motivated to succeed. However, problems arise when you try to do too much too fast and take on too much work.

This can lead to a drop in motivation, and it is no surprise that some studies estimate that as many as 9 out of 10 new gym members will have quit exercising within three months.

In chapter three, we will look at goal setting and how it can help you to find success with a balance exercise regime. In this chapter, we will take a look at practical steps you can take to ensure that your fitness journey defies the statistics and survives indefinitely.

Being prepared and knowing these simple tips can help you avoid common mistakes made by gym goers and ensure your safety.

Tips

1. **If in Doubt, Ask**
   This is so crucial. Even with every resource available, mastering an exercise or workout routine immediately is incredibly difficult. You are going to get stuck at some point. It may not be an exercise that stumps you. It may be an aspect of exercise.

   How long do you rest between sets? Can you take longer rest breaks if needed, or should you be super-strict? What should you do if you feel sick during a session?

   These questions may arise before you work out; don't worry, they will be covered in this book. But if you are unsure about something, it is always advisable to ask. You can ask people at the gym, ask for help online, or ask your doctor (if it is a medical question). Just don't think that you have to do everything on your own.

2. **Preparing Your Exercise Area**

   Safety is very important when exercising. This can involve the movement itself, the equipment you use, and the safety of others. But one area that people sometimes forget to consider is the area in which you are training.

   This is particularly important if you are training at home or in a local park. There are several reasons for this:

   - **Uneven surfaces** – You may lose your footing, or balancing exercises may be more challenging. If you are placing a chair down on this surface, you want it to be nice and flat and able to withstand your weight easily.
   - **Tripping hazards** – Check to make sure that there aren't things that can trip you up in your exercise area. If you are outside, then don't forget to check for roots, branches, or slippery surfaces such as mud.
   - **Other people** – You want to ensure that where you are exercising is not going to have a lot of foot traffic. If you are in your house, then let everyone know what you are doing first. If you

are in a park, then make sure that you are not near an entrance or in the middle of a path.

- **Equipment** – Is your equipment set up properly and securely? If you are using a chair, then is this chair stable? Will it move when you sit on it? Double-check this before using it.
- **Space** – The majority of exercises in this book will not take up much space. But you still want enough room to lie down properly with your arms and legs spread out. Make sure that you have the right amount of space to do this without hitting your arms or legs against furniture, doors, walls, or something similar.

This may all sound like a lot of tasks to perform before starting your workout, but provided you train in the same area each time, this task will become second nature within a week or so.

If you are in a gym, then things are a bit different. Depending on how busy the gym is when you are there, it will either be incredibly easy or quite challenging.

If you can train during the day, the gym should be pretty quiet, and it should be easy to find enough space and a stable surface to perform your exercises.

Training very early in the morning or during the evening rush can be quite challenging. This is because the gym can get packed. This means having to share equipment and space and an increased risk of people walking through your workout area without noticing.

There's not much you can do about this except choose your space wisely and keep your eyes open for any potential hazards. If you can, always try and train during quiet times in the gym.

3. **Warming Up**

   In chapter four, we will be going into detail on what precisely a warm-up should consist of. But in this section, we are discussing why warming up is essential.

   There is currently a lot of debate in the fitness world about how vital warm-ups are, with many pros now cautioning that warm-ups are overrated. Of course, there is some logic to this, but this advice is mainly aimed at men and women in their 20s and early 30s.

   If you are over 60 years old, you need an effective warm-up before starting any exercise program. This warm-up doesn't have to be very long, nor does it need to be intense, particularly if you are performing chair exercises or various low-impact bodyweight exercises, but don't go into any workout "cold".

If you train in a gym, 5-10 minutes on a cardio machine such as an elliptical trainer or recumbent bike should be a good start. A brisk walk followed by our warm-up routines (chapter 4) should suffice if you are training outdoors.

If you are training at home, something simple like walking up and down the stairs or marching on the spot could count as cardio, then follow one of our warm-up routines.

4. **Equipment Check**

This was covered slightly in tip #2 as part of checking your exercise area. But that was more to do with how it was situated. This check is about ensuring that the equipment is functioning correctly and that you know how to use it.

Again, this sounds a lot more complicated than it is. If you are using a chair, then check that the chair is sturdy and can take your weight easily. If you use dumbbells, ensure the ends are tightly attached to the handles. If you are using exercise machines, try them out on a lower weight before using them properly.

Exercise benches are always best double-checked before you lie on them. Make sure you know how to adjust them and that they are fully locked in place before you lie down or sit on them. You can also check to ensure the bench is on a stable surface.

A piece of equipment will rarely let you down, but avoiding it completely requires a little forethought.

5. **Rest Between Sets and Exercises**

There is a lot of conflicting information when it comes to rest between sets and exercises. Luckily, balance exercise workouts are fairly straightforward. As balance exercises are skill-based and technical, you want quite a bit of rest between sets. On the other hand, they may be quite easy (particularly at first) and may not require much rest.

Here are some rules for you to follow when it comes to sets:

- Very easy exercises = 45-60 seconds of rest between sets
- Easy exercises = 60 seconds rest between sets
- Medium exercises = 60-90 seconds rest between sets

- Hard exercises = 2-3 minutes rest between sets
- Very hard exercises = 3-5 minutes between sets

With exercises, you can rest for as long as you feel that you need to. This can range from 0 seconds to 5 minutes. As you get stronger and fitter, you may find that your need for rest between exercises is diminished. You want to be pushing your capabilities but not so far that your form suffers.

The important thing for rest periods is to listen to your body. How are you feeling? In fitness, we use something called the Rate of Perceived Exertion scale (RPE). It goes from 1 to 10:

- 1 = sitting down, very light activity, regular heart rate
- 2-3 = light activity, slightly raised heart rate
- 4-6 = moderate activity, you can still talk fluently while performing it, heart rate is elevated
- 7-8 = high activity, running, you struggle to talk fluently, heart rate is high

- 9 = near maximal activity. You cannot talk as it is too hard, and your heart rate is nearing its max
- 10 = Maximal intensity. You can only keep this up for a couple of seconds more

If you are exercising between 1-4 RPE, then you won't need much rest. If you are exercising at 5-7, you will need 1-2 minutes of rest. If you are exercising at 8 or above, then you will need at least 3 minutes of rest.

6. **Heart Rate, Breathing, and Signs of Fatigue**
You don't need to own a heart rate monitor, but if you have one, then it can be beneficial for establishing how hard you are working. A heart rate monitor combined with your RPE scale (see above) is one of the best ways to find out how hard you are training, whether you can go harder, or whether you need to reign things in a little.

The first thing you need to do is establish your maximum heart rate. This is easy to do; just minus your age from 220. For example, if you are 70 years old, your max heart rate is 150 beats per minute (220 – 70 = 150).

- So, if you are 70 years old and your heart rate is up near 150 beats per minute, then you would score a 10 on the RPE scale. This is maximum intensity.

- Light activity would cause your heart rate to beat slightly higher than normal, so if your average heartbeats per minute are 65, you could expect to see your heart rate rise to 70 or 75.
- Moderate activity would see your heart rate rise to the 90s, and near-maximal activity would see your heart rate reach close to your max.

Breathing rate is another way to measure how tired you are. If you read tip #5, you can see that many of the descriptions talk about you being able to speak. This is an excellent indicator of how hard you are training.

If you are sitting or walking at a leisurely pace, you can talk easily. But you will find talking impossible if you are sprinting at top speed. Jogging (moderate activity) can make talking tricky, but you should still be legible. But hiking up a steep hill will undoubtedly make you breathe heavily and prevent you from speaking at a normal pace.

Use your breathing as a gauge for how hard you are training. This can be easier than using your heart rate unless you have an easy-to-understand heart rate monitor.

Other signs of fatigue can include trouble thinking, nausea, muscle ache, joint pain, and decreases in performance.

It is important to note that many exercises require you to become fatigued. You are not supposed to be in your comfort zone. Otherwise, you will never make progress. But, being overly fatigued may lead to accidents or injury.

Balance training involves a lot of coordination and technique, so you can't be too exhausted. Using your heart rate and breathing rate or checking any signs of fatigue can help you assess whether you need to take a more extended rest between sets or even curtail your session.

7. **Assess Your Mobility (Low, Medium, High)**

A full mobility screen needs to be performed by a certified professional, and it is not something that you can easily perform yourself. But you do have a couple of options:

1. Ask a professional to assess you – Obviously the best option, but this will cost money and may take a while to set up.

2. Answer some simple questions to get a basic idea – If you know that you have mobility issues, then you can easily score yourself as having "low mobility".

The workouts in this book are split between low, medium, and high mobility. Of course, having high mobility is the best-case scenario. It means that you can perform pretty much any exercise and don't have any injuries.

Medium mobility means that you may have one or two minor mobility issues, your shoulders don't move like they used to, or you have recently recovered from an old knee issue, which can be a little stiff. But most parts of your body move freely and without pain.

Low mobility means that you have had many injuries in the past or lifestyle factors that have caused you to struggle with simple movements. If you have low mobility, most exercises will be too difficult to perform (at least initially), meaning that your workout program will have to be simple.

Some people have so many mobility issues that a book won't be able to help them. If you can't walk (for example) or have an active injury/disability, you need to talk to a doctor or a physiotherapist. They can advise you on what action to take.

Bring the book with you, and they can approve/disapprove each exercise.

By now, you should know what you need to do before starting your first workout. You should understand the importance of asking questions when unsure of something and how to safely prepare your exercise area, whether outside, at home, or in the gym. You should also know how to inspect your equipment before using it to ensure it isn't damaged or incorrectly set up.

You should also have a good idea of how long to rest between sets, how to tell whether you are fatigued and whether you have low, medium, or high mobility. Use this chapter to double-check just before each workout. After a while, these steps will come naturally to you, and you will barely notice that you are doing them.

Now that we've sorted this out, we can move on to the next chapter, where we will be discussing goal setting. You will learn how to create effective goals, measure your progress, and assess how well you are doing.

CHAPTER 3

Goal Setting

"Goals give us purpose, which, in turn, motivates us to make ourselves the best version in all aspects of our life."

Hannah Bronfman

The key to success in any endeavour is to create realistic and effective goals, ensure that each goal is achievable, and then measure your progress as you go along. Embarking on an exercise program should always start with proper goal setting, yet it is one of the most overlooked steps.

In this chapter, you will learn the importance of effective goal setting, how to create realistic goals, what SMART goals are, and how to measure your progress throughout your exercise program.

The Importance of Setting Realistic Goals

Motivation is important for anyone who is trying to exercise regularly. Contrary to popular belief, it is not essential, but it is important. Many people have achieved their goals without being motivated, but a motivated person is more likely to enjoy the process and achieve their goals.

Another misconception about motivation is that reading motivational messages or consuming motivational media is the best way to stay motivated. These can help some people, but most people will be put off.

Real motivation comes from setting yourself mini-goals and then achieving them. For example, let's say that your overall goal is to run a marathon. It's no good writing "Run a marathon" on paper and then waiting for the motivation to kick in.

You need to break that goal down into smaller steps. Start with "run continuously for 200 metres", then increase the distance once you have achieved this goal.

But for these goals to be achieved, they have to be realistic. Running a marathon may be realistic for some, but for most people, it is unrealistic. If walking to the bus stop is challenging, then running over 26 miles is unlikely. Not impossible, but the odds may be stacked against you.

A more realistic goal for a senior might be to walk for 5 miles without having a rest. But, of course, you want the goal to be challenging and even a little inspiring. So this goal might not be perfect.

How to Create Realistic Goals

We touched on this briefly in the previous section, but one of the biggest mistakes people make is creating unrealistic goals. It's an easy mistake to make, partly because many of us overestimate our fitness and mobility levels (many of us also tend to underestimate them, but that's another issue entirely).

Before creating any goals, you need to know your current abilities. We will talk about this later on in the chapter.

- Step One: Assess current abilities
- Step Two: Create a timeframe
- Step Three: Aim for an achievable improvement in that time
- Step Four: Break that goal into smaller goals

Using our low, medium, or high mobility scores, you can assess your current abilities. Then give yourself a timeframe of 12 weeks to improve your mobility.

This aspect of goal setting doesn't suit mobility training or balance exercises perfectly, not in the same way it suits running or weight lifting. So, we can change the goals slightly.

Instead of focusing on the outcome (better balance), we can focus on the process. The workouts in this book are 30-days long, with training 3-4 times per week. So a realistic goal might be to train 16 times within 30 days.

This is realistic, and it is easy to measure. It also has a timeframe. If you had set a target of exercising 30 times within 30 days, you might have found this too difficult to achieve. On the other hand, if you had set a target of 2 training sessions in 30 days, you would accomplish the goal too easily.

Another way to create realistic goals is to perform balance tests. These aren't exercises. They are used purely to measure your progress. At the end of this chapter, we will look at three balance tests for you to perform at the start of your training program, halfway through, and at the end.

You can use the results of the initial tests to create realistic goals for the program.

What are SMART Goals

SMART goals were created by George T. Doran in 1981 and were initially designed to develop goals for businesses. But they fit perfectly with fitness and nutrition and have been widely adopted.

SMART stands for specific, measurable, attainable, relevant, and time-based, and for a goal to be considered effective, it should fit all five criteria. This section will discuss each criterion and then provide an example of a SMART goal for fitness.

Specific

Vague goals are tough to measure and assess. "I want to have better balance" is admirable, but how do you measure it? Via testing. This is why balance tests are so necessary. Use the test to create a specific goal. For example, I scored (x) in pre-training and would like to score (y) after 30 days.

If you were trying to run a marathon, then a specific goal would not be "I want to run a marathon"; it would be "I want to run a marathon in under 3 hours within six months. My current time is 4 hours".

Measurable

Ensuring that your goals can be measured before, during, and after your training program is also crucial. But, again, with balance exercises, this comes down to specific tests.

In fitness, goals can be measured based on the weight you are lifting (resistance training) or how long it takes you to run a certain distance. You can also get physique goals (how much your biceps grow by, for example). Or how much weight you gain/lose over time.

Attainable

This is just another word for realistic. Are your goals attainable? There is no point in setting yourself a goal to run a sub-10 second 100 metres because unless you are a professional sprinter at the top of your game, you will not achieve it.

Relevant

This book aims to improve your balance, so setting a goal that you want to lose 10 lbs is not a good idea because it is not relevant to what you are hoping to achieve.

Time-Based

Open-ended goals can sometimes work, but setting a realistic deadline can significantly impact your chances of success. Setting a time-based goal grounds you in reality immediately. An untimed goal can be derailed by procrastination. It is also harder to make an untimed goal specific or measurable.

Example of a SMART Goal

Please read the Timed Up & Go test procedure (below) so that you can understand how it fits into this SMART Goal.

Pre-test: Perform the Timed Up & Go test. You manage 20 seconds.

You set your goal that in 30 days, you will be able to perform the test in 14 seconds, reducing your time by 6 seconds.

- Specific: The goal is focused on improving your balance during a balance test
- Measurable: The goal is based on the length of time it takes to perform the test in seconds
- Attainable: An average score for the Timed Up & Go test is around 14 seconds. Most people who train for 30 days should be able to achieve this.

- Relevant: The test measures balance, which is the goal of this book
- Time-Based: You have 30 days to complete this goal

Setting Baseline Stats

For this part, you are going to need a pen and paper. Baseline stats are used as a reference point to see how much you have improved over time. This book has two tests: the Timed Up & Go test and the one-legged stance test.

You will complete each test and write down your scores. Then you can use these stats to measure your progress after 15 days and after 30 days.

Measuring Progress

You want to measure progress regularly but must find the sweet spot between over-measuring and under-measuring. For example, if you test yourself daily, you may tire yourself before performing the workout. You might also find that you struggle mentally with the up-and-down nature of scores.

Progress is not linear, and you may see drops in performance when performing tests daily. That's why it is a good idea to space your tests out. Testing every two weeks (or 15 days) spreads the testing evenly and smooths out any variance in performance.

Keep a written record of your results in each test, and you can analyse how they are going over the course of a year.

Analysing Your Results

Luckily, both tests are very straightforward. You want to get your score as low as possible for the TUG test. With the OLST test, you want to get your scores as high as possible. This makes it easy to analyse progress.

You are making good progress if you scored 20 seconds the first time you performed the TUG test and 18 seconds the second time. However, if you scored 24 seconds the second time, then you are regressing. At some point, you will see that your scores peak and begin to flatline. Don't worry. This is perfectly acceptable for the TUG test, but keep testing to ensure that you aren't regressing.

Balance Tests for Seniors

In 2016, the Journal of Physical Therapy Science established the five best tests for balance in seniors [13]. It found that a combination of two to three tests was best. We've examined each test and found that only two can easily be performed without a professional analysing you.

These two tests are the Timed Up & Go Test (TUG) and the One-Legged Stance Test (OLST). Both tests are easy to learn, and while they are designed to be challenging, they don't require much technical knowledge or any specialist equipment.

All you will need to perform these tests are:

- One sturdy chair
- A tape measure
- Either some masking tape or something to mark a distance
- A stopwatch

Ideally, you would want somebody to help you by timing you during each test, but it is possible to do both tests alone, provided you have a clock that you can easily see.

Timed Up & Go Test (TUG)

Find a sturdy chair, and place it on a hard surface (no carpet). Then, with a tape measure and some masking tape, measure a 3-metre distance from the chair and place your tape down.

Sit down on the chair. All you have to do now is stand up, walk to the 3-metre mark, and then walk back to the chair and sit down. Start your stopwatch as soon as you climb out of the chair. Stop the stopwatch when you successfully sit down again. You can do this with a walking stick if needed.

Record your time. You can have one practice round before your timed test. A score of under 14 seconds (unaided) would represent someone with good mobility and balance. A score under 20 seconds (unaided) is medium, or a score under 14 seconds but with a walking stick.

A score over 20 seconds, or over 14 seconds with a walking stick, would rank as low mobility. But this is just a rough guide. It doesn't take into account upper-body mobility issues or balance issues.

One-Legged Stance Test (OLST)

You will need a flat surface (no carpet) and a stopwatch for this test. Someone to observe and use the stopwatch would also be helpful. This test is quite a bit longer, but it is more straightforward.

Stand upright. You may want to stand near a wall or table so that you can grab hold of it for support if needed. Place your hands across your chest so they can't be used for balance.

Raise one foot off the ground and bring it up until it is level with the ankle of your stationary foot. Hold this one-legged stance for as long as you can. When you can't hold it any longer, put your foot down and record your time.

Repeat this with your other foot, and record that time too.

Once you have done both feet, you are going to repeat the process, but this time you are going to do so with your eyes closed. Record your times.

Age	Ideal Score Eyes Open	Ideal Score Eyes Closed
60-69	27 seconds +	2 seconds +
70 +	18 seconds +	1 second +

Scores from a 1998 study by El-Kashlan *et al.* [14].

CHAPTER 4

Warm-Ups for Seniors

"A muscle is like a car. If you want to run well early in the morning, you have to warm it up."

Florence Griffith Joyner (Flo-Jo)

The older you are, the more important an effective warm-up becomes. In this chapter, we are going to look at warm-ups that you can perform in your home, outside (in a park, for example), or in the gym. We will also look at warm-ups that suit low-mobility, medium-mobility, and high-mobility.

These warm-ups are designed to complement a balance exercise workout, but they can also be used for regular workouts or before sporting events.

Home Warm-Ups

The main issue with warming up in your home is the lack of space available. If you have a cardio machine such as a treadmill or exercise bike, then you can use that. But these warm-ups are designed for homes that don't have any equipment.

Low-Mobility

If you have low mobility, then the best warm-up you can do at home will involve warming up the whole body, starting from your head and going down to your toes.

- **Neck warm-up**: Stand upright, looking straight forward. Slowly, bring your head backwards until you are looking up at the ceiling. Pause, and then bring your chin down towards your chest. Again, do this very slowly. Return your head to the starting position, then turn your head until your chin is looking over your right shoulder, bring it back, and then bring it over your left shoulder.
- **Shoulder and Upper Back warm-up**: Stand upright with your feet shoulder-width apart. Now you are going to raise your shoulders up towards your ears, hold this position briefly, and then slowly return them to the start. Do this five times. Next, you are

going to perform some shoulder rolls. This is where you bring your shoulders forward, then slowly roll them up into a shrug and then backwards. Again, do this five times.

- **Arm warm-up**: This is similar to arm circles but has been adapted to make the exercise more suited to low mobility. Stand upright with your arms by your side. Push your chest out and pull your shoulder blades backwards. Raise both arms up into the air, and pause when they are above your head (or as high as you can comfortably get them). Pause, and then lower them back down to the starting position.
- **High Knees** warm-up: For this exercise, you will want a chair to stand next to. Use the chair for balance. Stand upright with your chest pushed out. Raise one foot off the ground, bringing your knee up until your thigh is parallel to the floor. Pause, and then lower it back down. Repeat with your other leg. Perform 5-10 times with each leg.
- **Reverse Knees** warm-up: Stand against a wall, or use a chair for balance. Stand upright and bring your foot backwards and upwards towards your glutes. Pause when your lower leg is parallel to the floor, then lower back down. Repeat with your other leg. Perform 5-10 times with each leg.

- **Calf Raises** warm-up: Stand against a wall, or use a chair for balance. Stand upright with your chest pushed out. Raise your heels off the ground until you are on your tiptoes. Pause, and then lower your heels back down. Repeat ten times.

Exercise	**Sets**	**Reps**	**Rest Between Sets**
Neck Warm Up	1	6	n/a
Shoulder Shrugs	1	5	n/a
Shoulder Rolls	1	5	n/a
Arm Circles	1	10	n/a
High Knees	1 (each leg)	5-10	30 seconds
Reverse Knees	1 (each leg)	5-10	30 seconds
Calf Raises	1	10	n/a

SCAN FOR VIDEO

Medium-Mobility

If you have medium mobility, then you can still perform the same warm-up as the low-mobility, or you can perform some slightly more challenging versions of the previous exercises. Here are some examples of some more dynamic warm-ups that you can add to your low-mobility warm-up.

- **Arm Circles**: Stand upright with your arms by your side. Push your chest out and pull your shoulder blades backwards. Raise both arms up into the air. When they reach shoulder height, turn your hands out and continue to swing your arms so that they travel in a circle. Perform six rotations in one direction and then swap directions. If this feels painful, then return to performing the low-mobility version.
- **High Knees**: Stand upright with your chest pushed out. Raise one foot off the ground, bringing your knee up until your thigh is parallel to the floor. Pause, and then lower it back down. Repeat with your other leg. Perform 5-10 times with each leg. The difference between this and the low-mobility version is that you perform it at a faster pace.
- **Reverse Knees**: Use a chair for balance. Stand upright and bring your foot backwards and upwards

towards your glutes. Pause when your lower leg is parallel to the floor, then lower back down. Repeat with your other leg. As with the high knees variation, the only difference between this and the low-mobility reverse knees exercise is the pace you perform it at.

- **Stair Climbing**: If your house has a staircase and you have medium mobility, then simply climbing up and down the stairs a few times will serve as a fantastic cardio-based warm-up. You don't need to go particularly fast, but a brisk pace would be ideal.

Exercise	Sets	Reps	Rest Between Sets
Arm Circles	1 (each direction)	6	30 seconds
High Knees	1 (each leg)	5-10	30 seconds
Reverse Knees	1 (each leg)	5-10	30 seconds
Stair Climbing	1	30-60 seconds	n/a

High-Mobility

As with the medium-mobility warm-up, you can easily incorporate all of the previous exercises into a high-mobility warm-up. But you can also add in more challenging exercises to increase the difficulty and allow yourself more variety.

Only perform these exercises if you assess yourself as having high mobility. They can be highly effective, but they can also increase your risk of injury if you are not yet ready for them.

- **Jogging on the spot**: This is just a faster version of high knees. Ensure that your knees are nice and high as you jog briskly on the spot. You can place your hands out in front of you for balance or hold onto a chair if you need to.
- **Mountain Climbers**: Place both hands on the seat of a chair and get into a push-up position so that your body is at an angle. Keeping your upper body still, bring one knee towards your chest, then as you bring it back down, simultaneously bring your opposite knee towards your chest. Start slowly, and then increase the speed as you get comfortable with the movement. Perform this for 40-60 seconds.
- **Lateral Lunges**: Stand upright with your feet together and your chest pushed out. Take a large lateral step to the right, keeping your left leg straight as you do so. Slowly bend your right knee until you feel a stretch, and then return your right leg to the starting position. Repeat with your opposite leg. Perform ten reps on each side.

- **Bodyweight squats**: As a warm-up, you are focusing more on the movement than you are on tiring yourself out. So perform these reps slowly while paying attention to your range of movement throughout. Stand upright with feet shoulder-width apart, and your toes turned out slightly. Push your chest out and clasp your hands together like you are praying. Slowly lower your glutes towards the floor, ensuring that your heels are touching the floor throughout. Pause when your thighs are around parallel to the floor, then rise back up again slowly. Perform ten reps, have a rest, and then perform ten more.

Exercise	**Sets**	**Reps**	**Rest Between Sets**
Jogging on the Spot	1	30-60 seconds	n/a
Mountain Climbers	1	40-60 seconds	n/a
Lateral Lunges	1 (each leg)	10	30 seconds
Bodyweight Squats	2	10	30 seconds

Gym Warm-Ups

One of the reasons why gyms are so popular is the huge variety of machines and pieces of equipment they provide. Membership fees vary and can be quite expensive however, provided you use them regularly, they generally represent good value for money. However,

I strongly suggest find a gym which permits a trial membership before making an annual commitment or a gym which provides a monthly membership option. After a couple of months you can assess how frequently you use the gym and then assess whether membership makes financial sense.

The huge variety of equipment available makes warm-ups a lot easier, whether you have low mobility, medium mobility, or high mobility. Of course, you can still use all of the exercises from the home warm-ups; we've just added a few gym-based ones to the mix.

Low-Mobility

We've recommended the cross-trainer (also known as the elliptical) as the ideal cardio machine for a low-mobility warm-up. But it is not the only option. Treadmills are good for a brisk walk, recumbent bikes are popular, and regular exercise bikes may be possible, depending on your body.

- **Cross-Trainer**: This cardio machine is ideal for people with low mobility, as it is very low-impact and easy to learn. The only issue that you might have is getting on or off again. Ask a staff member to show you the safest method if you're concerned. A good cross-trainer warm-up should last around

5-7 minutes. This will warm up both your upper and lower body. You can then follow it up with the home workout mobility exercises (below).

- **Neck warm-up:** Stand upright, looking straight forward. Slowly, bring your head backwards until you are looking up at the ceiling. Pause, and then bring your chin down towards your chest. Again, do this very slowly. Return your head to the starting position, then turn your head until your chin is looking over your right shoulder, bring it back, and then bring it over your left shoulder.
- **Shoulder and Upper Back** warm-up: Stand upright with your feet shoulder-width apart. Now you are going to raise your shoulders up towards your ears, hold this position briefly, and then slowly return them to the start. Do this five times. Next, you are going to perform some shoulder rolls. This is where you bring your shoulders forward, then slowly roll them up into a shrug and then backwards. Again, do this five times.
- **Arm warm-up**: This is similar to arm circles but has been adapted to make the exercise more suited to low mobility. Stand upright with your arms by your side. Push your chest out and pull your shoulder blades backwards. Raise both arms up into the air, and pause when they are above

your head (or as high as you can comfortably get them). Pause, and then lower them back down to the starting position.

- **High Knees** warm-up: For this exercise, you will want a chair to stand next to. Use the chair for balance. Stand upright with your chest pushed out. Raise one foot off the ground, bringing your knee up until your thigh is parallel to the floor. Pause, and then lower it back down. Repeat with your other leg. Perform 5-10 times with each leg.
- **Reverse Knees** warm-up: Stand against a wall, or use a chair for balance. Stand upright and bring your foot backwards towards your glutes. Pause when your lower leg is parallel to the floor, then lower back down. Repeat with your other leg. Perform 5-10 times with each leg.
- **Calf Raises** warm-up: Stand against a wall, or use a chair for balance. Stand upright with your chest pushed out. Raise your heels off the ground until you are on your tiptoes. Pause, and then lower your heels back down. Repeat ten times.

Exercise	**Sets**	**Reps**	**Rest Between Sets**
Cross Trainer	1	5-7 minutes	n/a
Neck Warm Up	1	6	n/a
Shoulder Shrugs	1	5	n/a

Exercise	Sets	Reps	Rest Between Sets
Shoulder Rolls	1	5	n/a
Arm Circles	1	10	n/a
High Knees	1 (each leg)	5-10	30 seconds
Reverse Knees	1 (each leg)	5-10	30 seconds
Calf Raises	1	10	n/a

Medium-Mobility

This medium-mobility warm-up is going to be almost identical to the at-home medium-mobility warm-up, but instead of getting your cardio from a brisk walk or jog, you can get it from a cross trainer or any other form of cardio machine that suits your capabilities.

- **Cross-Trainer**: This cardio machine is ideal for people with low mobility, as it is very low-impact and easy to learn. The only issue that you might have is getting on or off again. Ask a staff member to show you the safest method if you're concerned. A good cross-trainer warm-up should last around 5-7 minutes. This will warm up both your upper and lower body.
- **Arm Circles**: Stand upright with your arms by your side. Push your chest out and pull your shoulder blades backwards. Raise both arms up into the air. When they reach shoulder height, turn your

hands out and continue to swing your arms so that they travel in a circle. Perform six rotations in one direction and then swap directions. If this feels painful, then return to performing the low-mobility version.

- **High Knees**: Stand upright with your chest pushed out. Raise one foot off the ground, bringing your knee up until your thigh is parallel to the floor. Pause, and then lower it back down. Repeat with your other leg. Perform 5-10 times with each leg. The difference between this and the low-mobility version is that you perform it at a faster pace.
- **Reverse Knees**: Use a tree, lamppost, or bench for balance. Stand upright and bring your foot backwards towards your glutes. Pause when your lower leg is parallel to the floor, then lower back down. Repeat with your other leg. As with the high knees variation, the only difference between this and the low-mobility reverse knees exercise is the pace you perform it at.

Exercise	**Sets**	**Reps**	**Rest Between Sets**
Cross Trainer	1	5-7 minutes	n/a
Arm Circles	1 (each direction)	6	30 seconds
High Knees	1 (each leg)	5-10	30 seconds
Reverse Knees	1 (each leg)	5-10	30 seconds

High-Mobility

There is a temptation to go all guns blazing with the high-mobility warm-up in the gym. There are so many options available. However, the point of a warm-up is to get your body prepared to train, not to exhaust yourself with a fancy warm-up. As with the other warm-ups in this section, it will be very similar to the outdoor and home high-mobility warm-ups, but with the addition of a cardio machine.

- **Treadmill Walking**: The high-mobility warm-up is more intense than others, so we'll keep the initial cardio section simple and just walk gently on a treadmill.
- **Gentle Burpees**: The burpee gets a lot of hate, but when performed correctly, it can warm up the whole body. Start in the push-up position, with hands shoulder-width apart and feet close together. Bring one knee towards your chest and place your foot down, then repeat with the other leg until you are in a crouched position. Now, carefully stand up until you are fully upright. This is one rep. Reverse the movement and get back into the starting position.
- **Sumo Squats**: This is a great variation of regular bodyweight squats, and it can really warm up the

lower body. Stand upright with your feet wider than shoulder-width apart. You really want your feet to be nice and wide. Now, slowly lower your glutes towards the floor, keeping your heels flat on the ground throughout. If you find that your heels are rising, then swap to a regular squat. Once your legs are parallel with the ground, rise back up again.

- **Lateral Lunges**: Stand upright with your chest pushed out and shoulders back. Place both of your feet together, then take a large step to the right, straightening your left leg and bending your right knee slightly. Pause, then return to the starting position. Repeat, using the opposite leg. Perform ten reps on each side.
- **Mountain Climbers** (Slow/Medium Speed): This is a great way to warm yourself up, and it can help you to get light on your feet. Place your hands on a bench or wall. If you can't find one, then you can place your hands on the floor and get into a push-up position. But it works best with a bench. Push your chest out, then slowly bring your left knee in towards your chest, pause and then return it. As you are doing so, bring your right knee into your chest. Start off slowly, and then raise the intensity as you go. Perform for 30-40 seconds.

- **Body Get-Ups**: Lie chest down on the floor with your legs straight. Now, all you have to do is stand up. Once you are fully upright, slowly return to the starting position. This exercise sounds so easy on paper, but try performing five reps in a row, and your heart will be racing! Vary the intensity based on your fitness. Remember, this is a warm-up, not the main workout.

Exercise	**Sets**	**Reps**	**Rest Between Sets**
Treadmill Walking	1	5 minutes	n/a
Gentle Burpees	1	10	n/a
Sumo Squats	1	10	n/a
Lateral Lunges	1 (each leg)	10	30 seconds
Mountain Climbers	1	30-40 seconds	n/a
Body Get Ups	2	5	30 seconds

CHAPTER 5

Chair Exercises

"Motivation gets you started but habit keeps you going."

F. Dupleix

Chair exercises are a fantastic way for people to improve their balance in a safe and secure manner. If you are training at home, then a sturdy chair is perfect. If you are training in a gym, then you can use an exercise bench or a plyometric box (though the bench is a better option).

You want to find a seat that is as stable as possible. Many advanced balance exercises are often based around instability, but those exercises are highly advanced and outside the scope of this book.

In this chapter, we will take a look at why chair-based exercises are so beneficial, how to find the right chair, how to progress your chair exercises as your balance improves, and what other equipment may be beneficial.

Five Benefits of Chair Exercises

This whole chapter is dedicated to chair-based exercises, so we obviously believe that chairs are an effective tool. But what are the benefits of chair exercises? Here are five of the biggest benefits:

1. **Accessible:** Most exercises require you to have a clean bill of health to perform them properly. They are not particularly accessible for people with mobility issues. Obviously, an Olympic weightlifting move is going to be inaccessible, but even a standing barbell bicep curl can be difficult for people with balance issues.

   Chair exercises are great because they can take away many of the barriers for some people to exercise. Have trouble standing? There is a chair-based alternative available. Chair exercises can also help with people who may have weakened muscles or a lack of flexibility in certain muscles.

They are perfect for introducing older people to the gym as they are safe and stable. We will discuss the confidence benefit more during benefit #3.

2. **Perfect for Limited Spaces:** Ideally, we'd all have the space for a huge in-home gym, but this is not realistic for most people. Equipment that looks small in a commercial gym can be way too big for home workouts. Whereas a chair? That piece of furniture is not only small and perfect for small spaces, but it can also be tidied away easily as it is a functional piece of furniture.
3. **Inexpensive:** Chairs themselves are not particularly cheap to purchase. But there are very few people who don't have access to a chair already. What are you sitting on now while reading this book? Ideally, you want a straight-backed wooden chair as this is the best for exercising on. But if you don't have that, then using a sofa or even a bed is possible.
4. **Great for Building Confidence:** There are very few people who will walk into a room, see a chair, and run away screaming. Chairs are safe and secure, and most people will trust them. This is important because a lot of gym equipment is intimidating, particularly to new users.

Even an exercise bench, which is in many ways safer and more effective than a chair, can look quite intimidating at first. They have odd adjustable settings, if they aren't properly locked in place, then they can fall down, and there's often a queue of people waiting for them to become available.

This is rarely the case with the humble chair. You can also perform chair exercises from the comfort of your own home, another confidence-boosting benefit.

5. **Versatile:** As you are about to find out in this chapter, there are a huge variety of chair exercises to learn, and many of them have a large number of variations. Meaning that you could perform a full workout with just a chair (and perhaps a couple of other pieces of equipment if you're feeling ambitious).

Finding the Right Chair

Look, if you only have one chair and you can't afford another one, then that is the chair for you. But there are certain chairs that are a better option for exercising on. Here are some criteria:

- **Straight-Backed** – You want your chair to have a straight back as it will help you to perform exercises such as seated shoulder presses. You can use the back to keep you upright without overworking your core muscles.

- **Reasonably Comfortable** – You want a chair that is comfortable but not *too* comfortable. Sitting on it should not be painful, and you don't want it to prevent you from exercising. But, nor do you want to be reclining in a comfy leather chair. This is supposed to be a workout!
- **Sturdy** – There is nothing more panic-inducing than the sound of a large creek just as you raise a set of dumbbells over your head. Pick a chair that can comfortably sit you and any weight that you are holding.
- **No Armrests** – Armrests can prevent you from performing a number of exercises properly. It's best to avoid chairs with armrests if you can.
- **No Wheels** – This feels obvious, but you know that if we don't mention the fact that your chairs shouldn't be mobile, somebody is going to do it.

Progressing Your Chair Exercises

There will come a point where the exercises that at one point felt so difficult will become simple and easy to use. So how do you progress with a chair exercise? Buy a bigger chair? Not quite.

- Increase mobility – This can come in a number of guises. An extreme example would be changing from a normal box squat into a one-legged box squat. By lifting one foot off the floor, you are making the exercise a lot more difficult without having to add any equipment.
- Increase the volume – Perform more reps or more sets. Instead of performing ten box squats, perform two sets of 12 box squats.
- Change the tempo – Speeding up or slowing down an exercise can make it easier or harder. Increasing the speed that you run obviously makes it more challenging. But slowing down a dumbbell bicep curl (for example) can make it much more difficult. This can work well with chair-based exercises.
- Add resistance – Finding your box squats easy? Why not hold a dumbbell in each hand while performing them? Are your seated leg extensions flying by? What if you attach a resistance band to your ankle? Much more challenging.

Optional Equipment

You don't need anything other than a chair to perform most of the exercises on this list. But a set of light/ medium dumbbells could be very useful. A couple of resistance bands could also really help. You can also use a kettlebell or medicine ball for some variations. Ankle weights are great for one or two exercises and are very cheap to buy.

The program is designed for people who only own a single chair, but if you want to progress, then small investments in fancy exercise equipment could be really effective.

30 Chair Exercises

Here are thirty chair exercises. You don't need to learn all of them. Some of them will be unsuitable for you, either too easy or too hard.

Each exercise on this list will be labelled: Low, Medium, or High Mobility. This way, you can perform exercises that are suited to your capabilities. Some exercises will require dumbbells or resistance bands, but if you don't have either, you can still create a superb program.

Chair Exercise #1 Box Squat

Mobility Rating: Low

Muscles Worked: Glutes, hamstrings, quadriceps, core muscles

How to Perform:

1. Stand in front of a chair with feet shoulder-width apart and toes turned out very slightly.
2. Take a deep breath, push your chest out, pull your shoulders back, and slowly lower your glutes until they touch the seat.
3. Pause, then rise back up again, breathing out as you go.

Tips: Try to avoid bouncing off the chair, but don't rest too long, either. Sit down, then rise back up again. You also want to ensure that your heels stay flat on the floor throughout this movement.

SCAN FOR VIDEO

Chair Exercise #2 Box Squat with Hands Behind Head or Raised Above Head

Mobility Rating: ***Medium***

Muscles Worked: Glutes, hamstrings, quadriceps, core muscles, deltoids, traps

---

How to Perform:

1. Stand in front of a chair with feet shoulder-width apart and toes turned out very slightly. Place your hands behind your head, interlocking your fingers.
2. Take a deep breath, push your chest out, pull your shoulders back, and slowly lower your glutes until they touch the seat. Keep your hands above your head throughout the movement.
3. Pause, then rise back up again, breathing out as you go.

Tips: This exercise will really work your core muscles and will make balancing a lot more difficult. It's a great progression but best suited to people with medium or high mobility.

SCAN FOR VIDEO

Chair Exercise #3 Box Squat with Dumbbell

Mobility Rating: **Medium**

Muscles Worked: Glutes, hamstrings, quadriceps, core muscles

How to Perform:

1. Stand in front of a chair with feet shoulder-width apart and toes turned out very slightly.
2. Hold a dumbbell sideways (so that it resembles an hourglass or goblet) so that it is just in front of your chest.
3. Take a deep breath, push your chest out, pull your shoulders back, and slowly lower your glutes until they touch the seat.
4. Pause, then rise back up again, breathing out as you go.

Tips: The dumbbell's main function in this exercise is to help you to keep your chest up. If your chest drops, then the weight will sag, helping you to realise what is happening. The weight can also increase the resistance.

SCAN FOR VIDEO

Chair Exercise #4 Box Squat into Shoulder Press (Dumbbells)

Mobility Rating: **High**

Muscles Worked: Glutes, hamstrings, quadriceps, core muscles, deltoids, traps

---

How to Perform:

1. Stand in front of a chair with feet shoulder-width apart and toes turned out very slightly.
2. Hold a dumbbell in each hand, resting at shoulder height with your palms facing each other.
3. Take a deep breath, push your chest out, pull your shoulders back, and slowly lower your glutes until they touch the seat.
4. Pause, then rise back up again, breathing out as you go. As you do so, raise the dumbbells up above your head until your arms are almost fully extended.
5. Lower them back down, and then sit back down to continue the exercise.

Tips: This exercise is incredibly taxing on the cardiovascular system, which makes it great for burning calories and improving your fitness. But you may find it very challenging, even if you have excellent mobility.

SCAN FOR VIDEO

Chair Exercise #5 Single Leg Box Squat

Mobility Rating: (very) **High**

Muscles Worked: Glutes, hamstrings, quadriceps, core muscles

How to Perform:

1. Stand in front of a chair with feet shoulder-width apart and toes turned out very slightly.
2. Take a deep breath, push your chest out, and pull your shoulders back.
3. Raise your left leg off the floor and slowly lower your glutes until they touch the seat.
4. Pause, then rise back up again, breathing out as you go.
5. Repeat the movement for several reps and then swap feet.

Tips: This will work your balance more than any other exercise, and it will really work your core. The single-leg box squat is incredibly challenging. Use your arms for balance, and only attempt when you feel that you are ready.

SCAN FOR VIDEO

Chair Exercise #6 Seated Leg Extension

Mobility Rating: **Low**

Muscles Worked: Quadriceps

How to Perform:

1. Sit on the edge of your chair, with your chest pushed out and shoulders back. Both feet should be flat on the floor. Hold onto the sides of the chair with your hands.
2. Slowly raise one leg up until your thigh is parallel with the floor (or as high as you can manage)
3. Pause and squeeze the muscle, then slowly lower it back down.
4. Repeat ten times and then swap legs

Tips: This exercise works best when performed slowly and with purpose. Don't just kick your leg out, be controlled in your movement. This is true for almost any exercise, but particularly so for leg extensions.

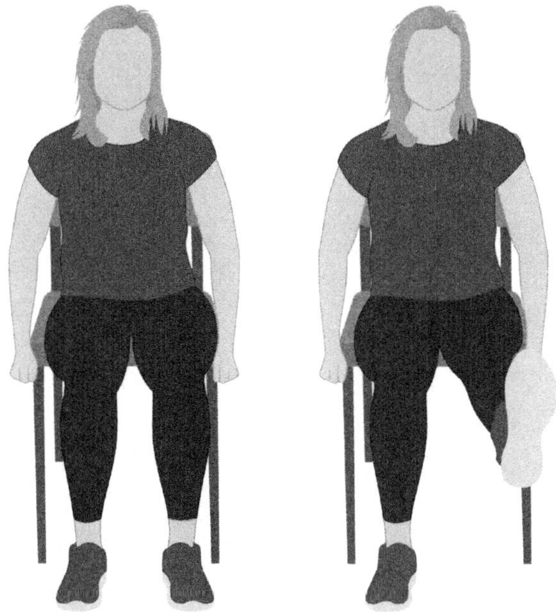

SCAN FOR VIDEO

Chair Exercise #7 Seated Leg Extension with Ankle Weights

Mobility Rating: **Low**

Muscles Worked: Quadriceps

How to Perform:

1. Sit on the edge of your chair, with your chest pushed out and shoulders back. Both feet should be flat on the floor. Hold onto the sides of the chair with your hands.
2. Attach an ankle weight to the leg that is about to be extended
3. Slowly raise one leg up until your thigh is parallel with the floor (or as high as you can manage)
4. Pause and squeeze the muscle, then slowly lower it back down.
5. Repeat ten times and then swap legs

Tips: Ankle weights are a great way to improve your balance and increase the difficulty of certain exercises. They don't need to be too heavy. Even a small ankle weight will feel heavy during a leg extension.

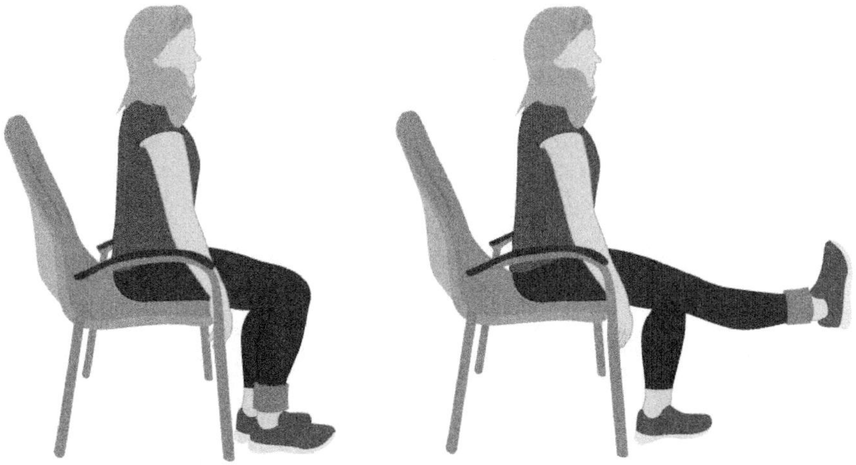

SCAN FOR VIDEO

Chair Exercise #8 Seated Leg Extension with Resistance Band

Mobility Rating: **Medium**

Muscles Worked: Quadriceps

How to Perform:

1. Sit on the edge of your chair, with your chest pushed out and shoulders back. Both feet should be flat on the floor. Hold onto the sides of the chair with your hands.
2. Your right foot should have a resistance band wrapped around it
3. The other end of the resistance band should be firmly attached to a secure piece of furniture. If the resistance band is short, then you can use the leg of the chair as an anchor
4. Slowly raise one leg up until your thigh is parallel with the floor (or as high as you can manage)
5. Pause and squeeze the muscle, then slowly lower it back down.
6. Repeat ten times and then swap legs

Tips: Finding the right size resistance band is important here. You want it to be light/medium. Too heavy, and you won't be able to raise your legs to parallel. This exercise can also be performed with both legs being lifted simultaneously.

SCAN FOR VIDEO

SCAN FOR VIDEO

Chair Exercise #9 Seated Leg Extension with Abduction

Mobility Rating: **Medium**

Muscles Worked: Quadriceps, abductors

How to Perform:

1. Sit on the edge of your chair, with your chest pushed out and shoulders back. Both feet should be flat on the floor. Hold onto the sides of the chair with your hands.
2. Slowly raise one leg up until your thigh is parallel with the floor (or as high as you can manage)
3. Pause and squeeze the muscle.
4. Instead of lowering it, bring it out to the side slightly
5. Pause, then bring it back to the middle, and then slowly lower it back down
6. Repeat ten times and then swap legs

Tips: Don't overstretch your leg while abducting, particularly if you have hip issues. Be conservative, and build up your strength and flexibility over time.

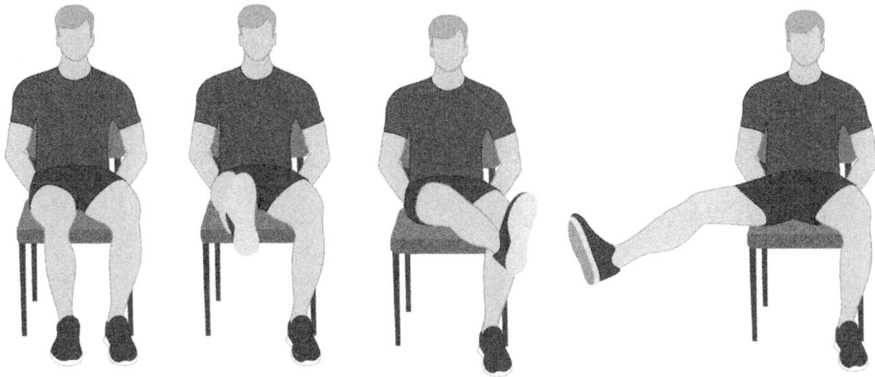

SCAN FOR VIDEO

Chair Exercise #10 Seated Leg Extension with Abduction (Ankle Weights)

Mobility Rating: **Medium**

Muscles Worked: Quadriceps, abductors

How to Perform:

1. Sit on the edge of your chair, with your chest pushed out and shoulders back. Attach ankle weights to feet. Both feet should be flat on the floor. Hold onto the sides of the chair with your hands.
2. Slowly raise one leg up until your thigh is parallel with the floor (or as high as you can manage)
3. Pause and squeeze the muscle.
4. Instead of lowering it, bring it out to the side slightly
5. Pause, then bring it back to the middle, and then slowly lower it back down
6. Repeat ten times and then swap legs

Tips: If you find that your range of motion is being affected by the ankle weights, then take them off. They may be light in weight, but even a tiny amount of weight can make the movement much more challenging.

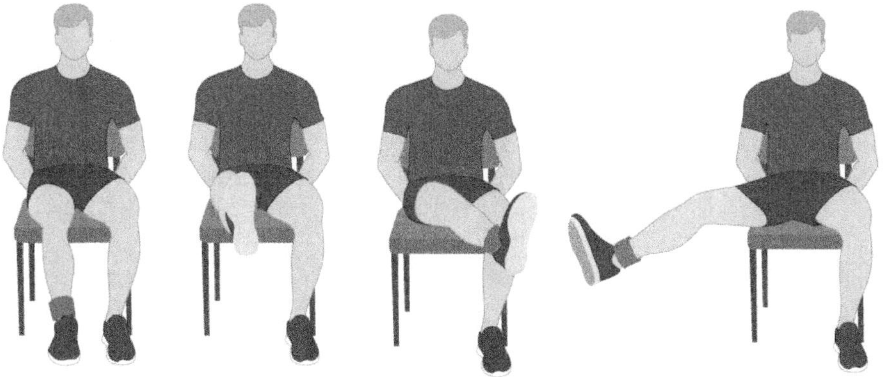

SCAN FOR VIDEO

Chair Exercise #11 Seated Calf Raises

Mobility Rating: **Low**

Muscles Worked: Calves

How to Perform:

1. Sit on the edge of your chair with feet shoulder-width apart and toes facing forward
2. Raise your heels off the ground, bringing your knees up as high as possible
3. Hold this position for a count of five, and then lower your heels back down to the floor

Tips: You can change this exercise by turning your toes inwards slightly or outwards. If you do three sets, then you can try once in each position.

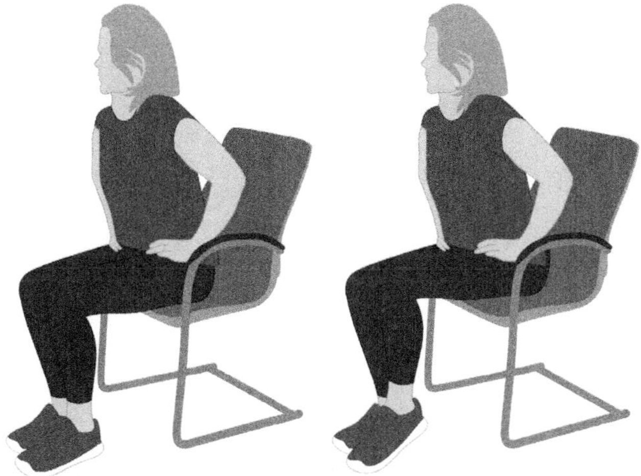

SCAN FOR VIDEO

Chair Exercise #12 Seated Calf Raises with Dumbbells

Mobility Rating: **Low**

Muscles Worked: Calves

How to Perform:

1. Sit on the edge of your chair with feet shoulder-width apart and toes facing forward
2. Place a dumbbell on each thigh just before it touches the knee
3. Raise your heels off the ground, bringing your knees up as high as possible
4. Hold this position for a count of five, and then lower your heels back down to the floor

Tips: If you find the dumbbells uncomfortable, then you could use your ankle weights instead. You don't need to try and attach them to your knees. Just rest them on top as a dead weight.

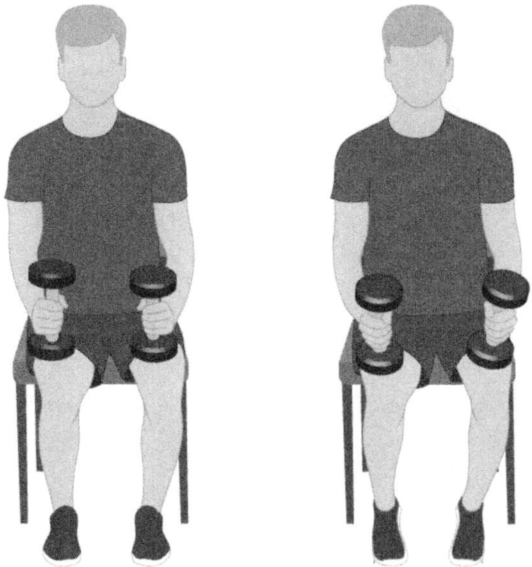

SCAN FOR VIDEO

Chair Exercise #13 Seated Hamstring Curls

Mobility Rating: **Low**

Muscles Worked: Hamstrings, quadriceps

How to Perform:

1. Sit on the edge of your chair with feet flat on the floor and shoulder-width apart.
2. Pull your feet backwards until your heels are as far back as possible
3. Pause, and then slowly bring your legs forward until your leg is straight in front of you with heels in the air.

Tips: This exercise will mostly work the hamstrings, but if you squeeze your quadriceps, you may also get a bit of quad-work in.

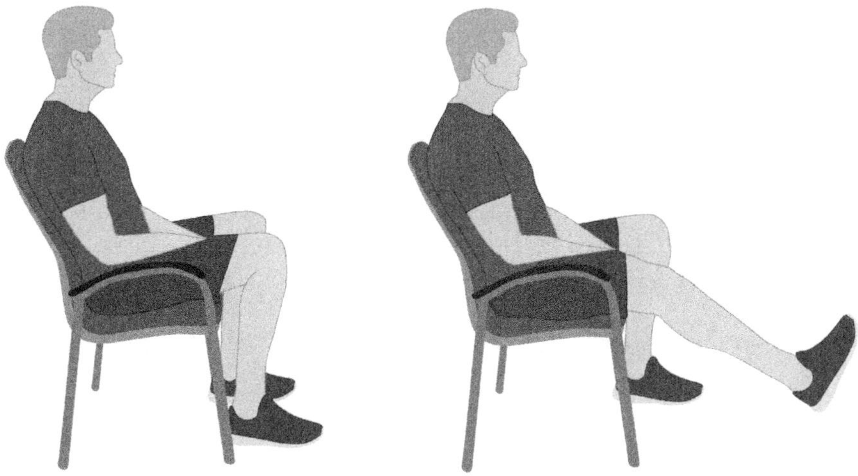

SCAN FOR VIDEO

Chair Exercise #14 Seated Hamstring Curls with Resistance Band

Mobility Rating: **Medium**

Muscles Worked: Hamstrings

How to Perform:

1. Set up a resistance band so that it is attached to a fixed point in front of your chair and draped around your heels.
2. Sit on the edge of your chair with feet flat on the floor and shoulder-width apart.
3. Pull your feet backwards until your heels are as far back as possible
4. Bring your legs forwards until your leg is straight out in front of you with heels in the air
5. Pause, and then return to the starting position

Tips: This exercise can be performed with one leg at a time instead if you prefer. Just ensure that the other foot is firmly rooted to the floor. You would also need to use a smaller resistance band.

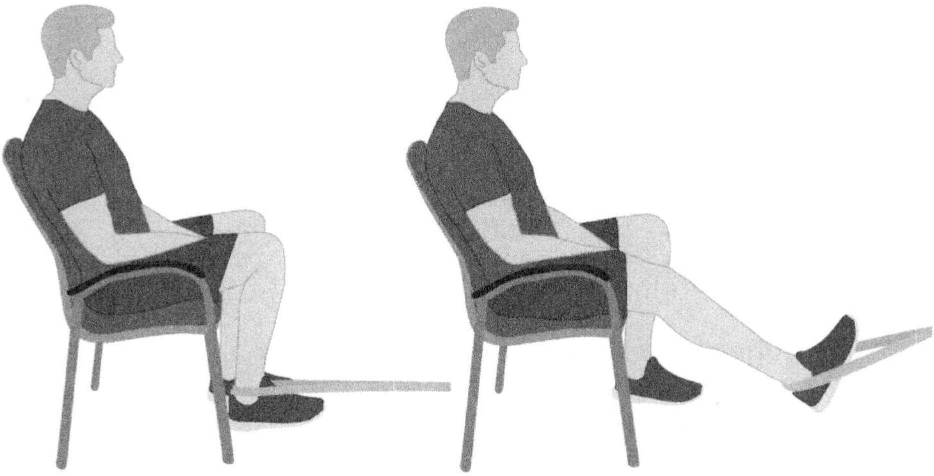

SCAN FOR VIDEO

Chair Exercise #15 Standing Hip Extension

Mobility Rating: **Low**

Muscles Worked: Glutes

How to Perform:

1. Stand behind a chair hold on tight.
2. With a straight leg (and pointed toes), bring your right leg back behind you
3. Pause, and then return your leg to the starting position
4. Perform ten reps and then swap legs (turn around so that your right hip is now close to the chair)

Tips: This exercise has a very short range of motion, and it is controlled. Do not swing your legs. Draw them backwards slowly.

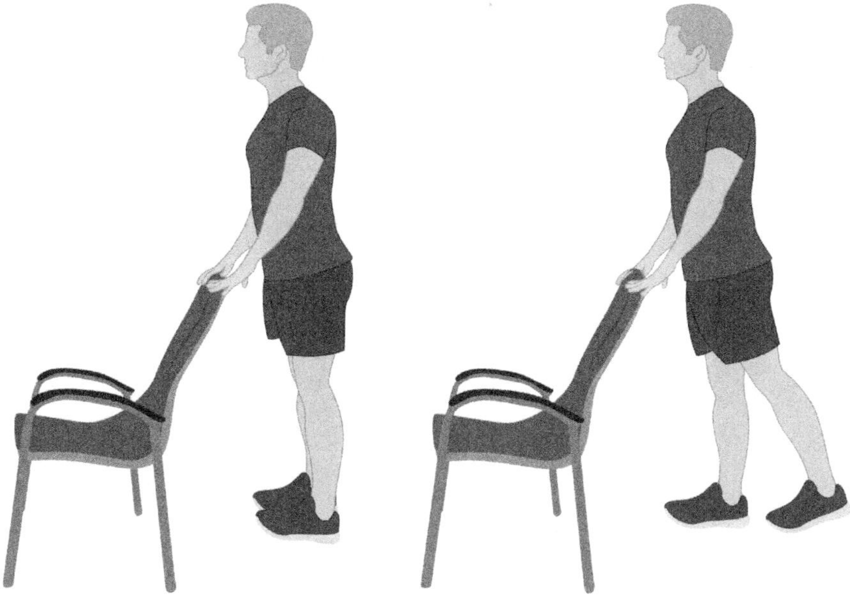

SCAN FOR VIDEO

Chair Exercise #16 Standing Hip Extension with Ankle Weights

Mobility Rating: **Low**

Muscles Worked: Glutes

How to Perform:

1. Place ankle weights on your legs
2. Stand behind a chair hold on tight.
3. With a straight leg (and pointed toes), bring your right leg back behind you
4. Pause, and then return your leg to the starting position
5. Perform 10 reps and then swap legs (turn around so that your right hip is now close to the chair)

Tips: This exercise is great for improving your balance, but the important thing is to stay in control. If the added weight makes it too hard, then revert to the regular version of this exercise.

SCAN FOR VIDEO

Chair Exercise #17 Single Leg Stand (Knee Forward)

Mobility Rating: **Low**

Muscles Worked: Quadriceps, hamstrings, glutes, core

How to Perform:

1. Stand behind a chair with both hands on the chair rest. Make sure that you are not too close to the chair
2. Using the chair for support, raise one knee in the air so that you are balancing on your remaining foot
3. Pause for up to 10 seconds (or just a couple of seconds if you are struggling), and then lower the foot back down
4. Repeat with the other foot

Tips: Try not to grip the chair too hard. The idea is that the chair is needed to help prevent you from falling. You may need to grip it hard at first, but as your balance improves, you can use a lighter and lighter grip until eventually being able to perform the exercise without a chair at all.

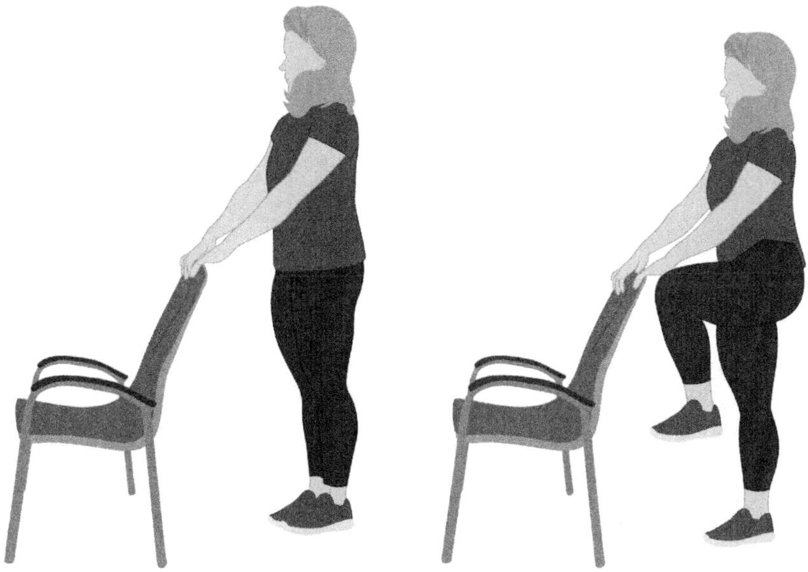

SCAN FOR VIDEO

Chair Exercise #18 Single Leg Stand (Heel Backwards)

Mobility Rating: **Low**

Muscles Worked: Quadriceps, hamstrings, glutes, core

How to Perform:

1. Stand behind a chair with both hands on the chair rest. Make sure that you are not too close to the chair
2. Using the chair for support, raise your heel back behind you in the air until your lower leg is parallel with the floor so that you are balancing on your remaining foot
3. Pause for up to 10 seconds, and then lower the foot back down
4. Repeat with the other foot

Tips: As your balance improves, you can begin to reduce your reliance on the chair until it can be removed completely.

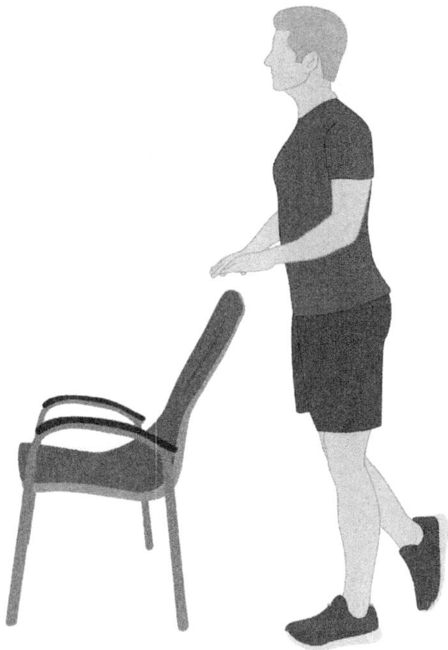

SCAN FOR VIDEO

Chair Exercise #19 Leg Swings (Forward & Back)

Mobility Rating: **Medium**

Muscles Worked: Glutes, quadriceps, hamstrings, core muscles

How to Perform:

1. Stand beside a chair so that your left hip is close to the chair. Hold on tight to the chair with your left hand.
2. With a straight leg (and pointed toes), swing your right leg back behind you
3. Once your leg has swung as far back as it can, swing it forwards as far forward as you can
4. Perform ten swings and then swap legs (turn around so that your right hip is now close to the chair)

Tips: You will find that the first swings are harder to perform. As you continue, your range of motion should increase. Don't try and force the swings.

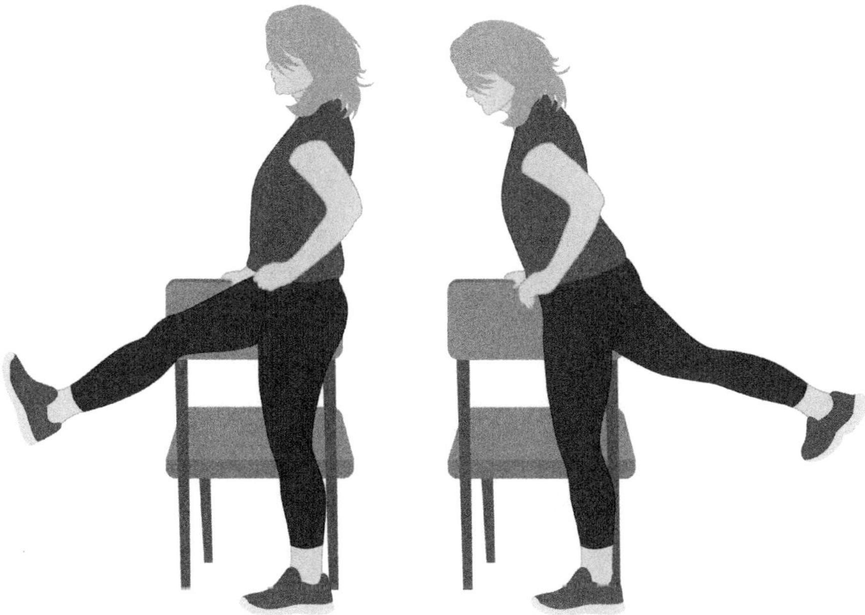

SCAN FOR VIDEO

Chair Exercise #20 Leg Swings (Side to Side)

Mobility Rating: **Medium**

Muscles Worked: Glutes, quadriceps, hamstrings, adductors, abductors, core muscles

---

How to Perform:

1. Stand behind a chair with both hands holding onto it
2. Lift one foot off the floor while keeping your leg straight and bring the raised foot across your standing leg
3. Keeping the leg straight, swing it out wide as far as you can
4. Swing it back in, finishing with your leg going past your standing leg
5. Repeat for ten swings and then swap legs

Tips: You will find that the first swings are harder to perform. As you continue, your range of motion should increase. Don't try and force the swings.

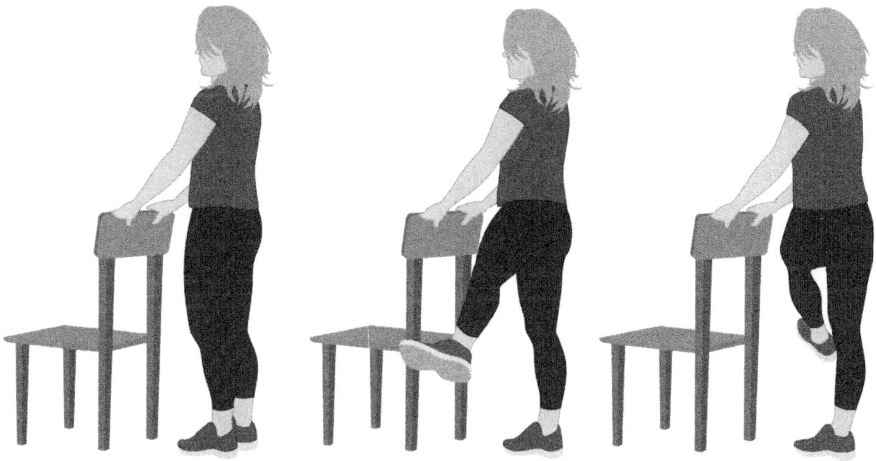

SCAN FOR VIDEO

Chair Exercise #21 Double Leg Lift

Mobility Rating: **Medium**

Muscles Worked: Core muscles, quadriceps

How to Perform:

1. Sit on a chair with your hands holding tight to the side of the seat
2. Simultaneously bring both legs up into the air
3. Pause, and then *slowly* lower them back down to the floor

Tips: This exercise will really work your abdominal muscles. Please do not attempt this on a chair with wheels, as you are likely to fly off it!

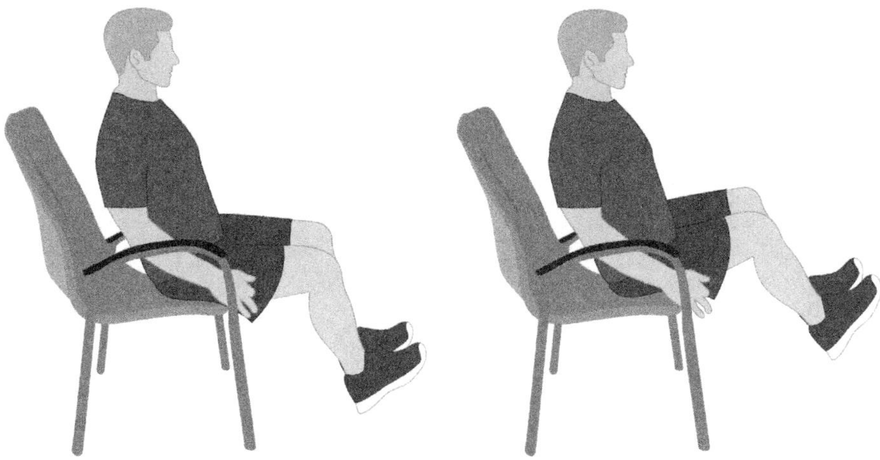

SCAN FOR VIDEO

Chair Exercise #22 Lateral Lunges

Mobility Rating: **Low**

Muscles Worked: Quadriceps, adductors, abductors, hamstrings, glutes

---

How to Perform:

1. Stand behind a chair so that you are sideways on. Your left hip should be brushing against the chair's back
2. Hold on to the back of the chair with your left hand, push your chest out and pull your shoulder blades back
3. Take a large step to the right, keeping your left foot in place. Bend your right knee and straighten your left leg so that you are leaning over your right knee.
4. Repeat ten times and then swap around. You should now be facing the opposite direction, with your right leg next to the back of the chair.

Tips: Keep your torso upright throughout this movement. Don't crouch over.

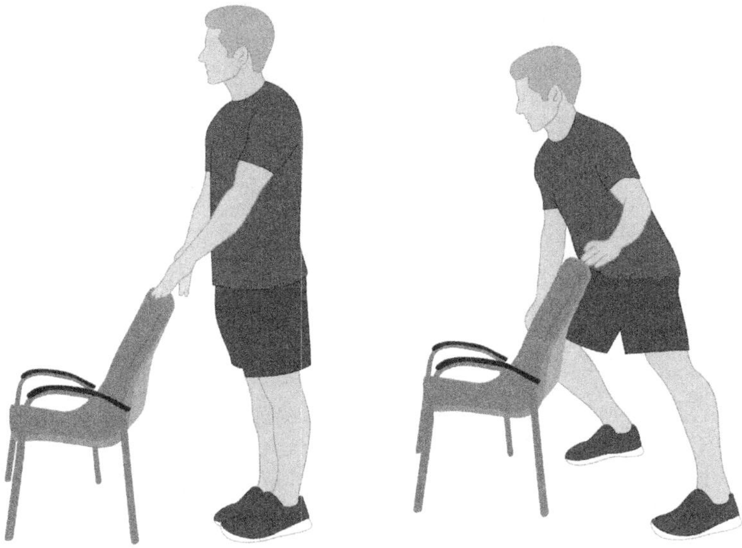

SCAN FOR VIDEO

Chair Exercise #23 Squats while Holding Chair

Mobility Rating: **High**

Muscles Worked: Glutes, hamstrings, quadriceps, core muscles

How to Perform:

1. Stand behind your chair with hands holding onto the back and your feet shoulder-width apart
2. Turn your toes out very slightly, push your chest out, and pull your shoulder blades backwards
3. Slowly lower your glutes towards the floor, using the chair for support
4. Pause when your thighs are nearly parallel to the floor

Slowly rise back up again

Tips: If you can get lower than parallel, then go for it. Try not to hold onto the chair too hard, as this can make the exercise awkward to perform.

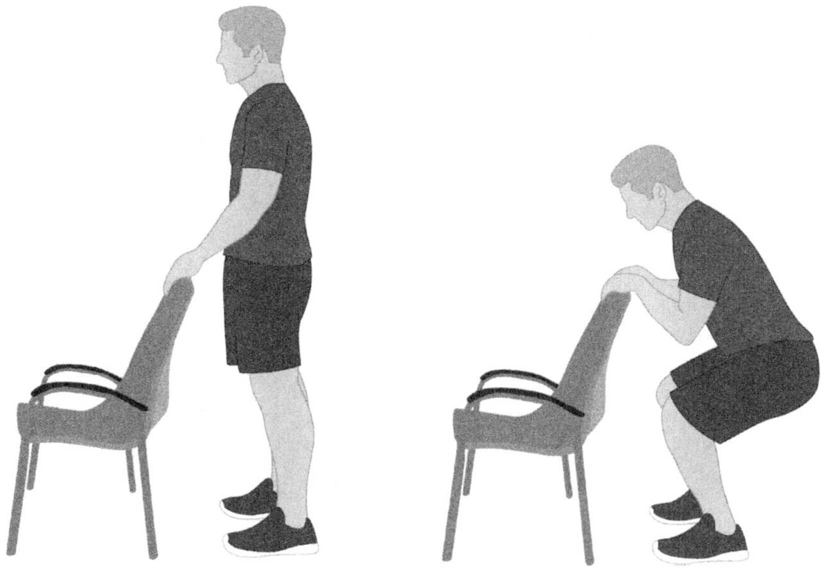

SCAN FOR VIDEO

Chair Exercise #24 Sumo Squats while Holding Chair

Mobility Rating: **High**

Muscles Worked: Glutes, hamstrings, quadriceps, core muscles

How to Perform:

1. Stand behind your chair with hands holding onto the back and your feet wider than shoulder-width apart
2. Turn your toes out very slightly, push your chest out, and pull your shoulder blades backwards
3. Slowly lower your glutes towards the floor, using the chair for support
4. Pause when your thighs are nearly parallel to the floor

Slowly rise back up again

Tips: The wide stance of a sumo squat can be very challenging and takes quite a bit of getting used to. Provided you have no hip issues. You should be fine. Just remember to keep a very wide stance and ensure your heels remain on the floor throughout.

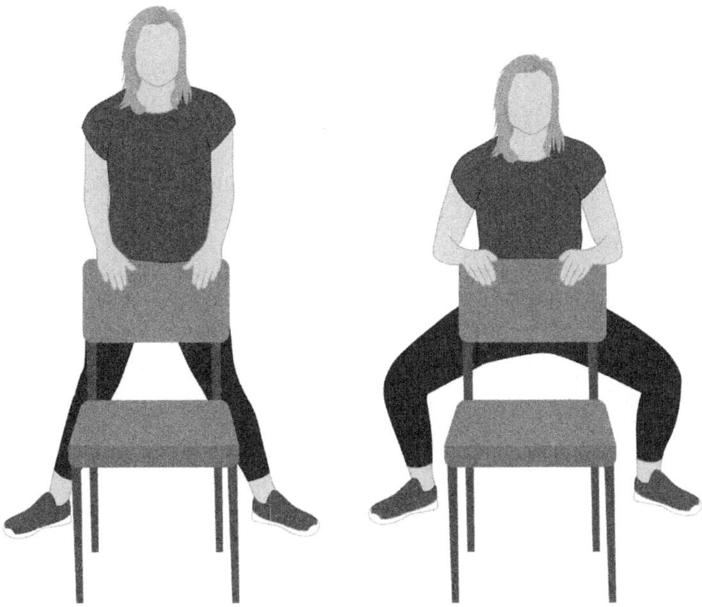

SCAN FOR VIDEO

Chair Exercise #25 Single-Leg Romanian Deadlift

Mobility Rating: **High**

Muscles Worked: Hamstrings, lower back, core muscles

How to Perform:

1. Stand behind a chair using the back for support, push your chest out and pull your shoulder blades back
2. Keep one leg nice and straight while raising the other foot off the floor
3. Keeping your leg straight, lean forwards as you bring your other foot backwards
4. You should feel a nice stretch in the back of your stationary leg
5. Perform ten reps and then swap legs

Tips: This exercise seems a lot more intimidating than it really is. The chair provides all the support that you need. The trick with this exercise is not to push your hamstrings too hard. Once you feel a decent stretch, stop and then return to the starting position. As your hamstrings get stronger and more flexible, you will be able to increase how far back your other foot goes.

SCAN FOR VIDEO

Chair Exercise #26 Sit and Reach

Mobility Rating: **Low**

Muscles Worked: Hamstrings

How to Perform:

1. Sit on the edge of your chair with one foot flat on the floor and your opposite leg straightened
2. Lean forwards and try to touch your toes
3. Once you have touched your toes (or gone as far forwards as you can), withdraw to the starting position.
4. Repeat with the other leg

Tips: This exercise is adapted from the sit and reach test, but it does a great job of strengthening and improving the flexibility of the hamstrings.

SCAN FOR VIDEO

Chair Exercise #27 Seated Elbow to Knee

Mobility Rating: **Medium**

Muscles Worked: Glutes, hamstrings, quadriceps, core muscles

How to Perform:

1. Sit on a chair with both feet flat on the floor
2. Raise your left knee up into the air
3. As you do so, bring your right elbow over until it touches your left knee
4. Return to the starting position and then repeat with your right knee and left elbow

Tips: You can make this more challenging by adding ankle weights. You can also perform it at a faster rate to increase the difficulty.

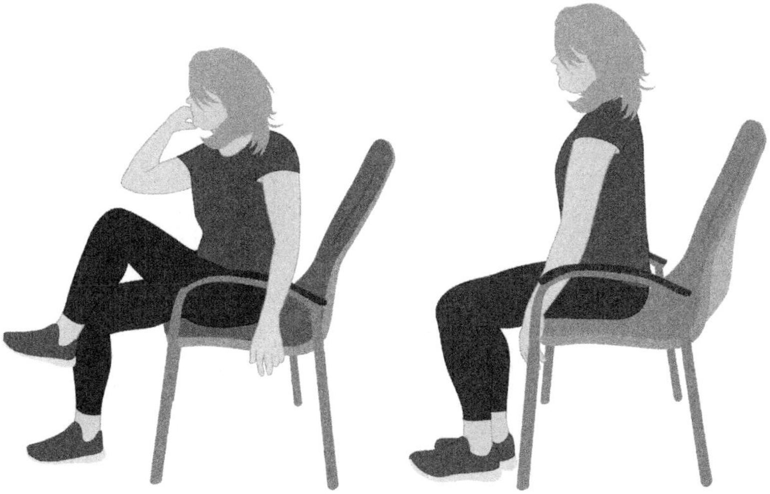

SCAN FOR VIDEO

Chair Exercise #28 Sumo Box Squat

Mobility Rating: **Medium**

Muscles Worked: Glutes, hamstrings, quadriceps, core muscles

How to Perform:

1. Stand in front of a chair with feet wider than shoulder-width apart and toes turned out very slightly.
2. Take a deep breath, push your chest out, pull your shoulders back, and slowly lower your glutes until they touch the seat.
3. Pause, then rise back up again, breathing out as you go.

Tips: The wide stance will place emphasis on the muscles of your inner and outer thigh, making the exercise feel more challenging than a regular box squat.

SCAN FOR VIDEO

Chair Exercise #29 Seated Resistance Band Bicep Curl

Mobility Rating: **Low**

Muscles Worked: Biceps

How to Perform:

1. Sit on a chair with a resistance band under your feet, with each end held in your hands
2. With your arms fully extended, curl your arms, bringing your hands up towards your shoulders
3. Squeeze your biceps and then slowly lower them back down to the starting position

Tips: Keep your elbows close to your sides throughout, and try to prevent them from moving too much. Let your biceps do all the work.

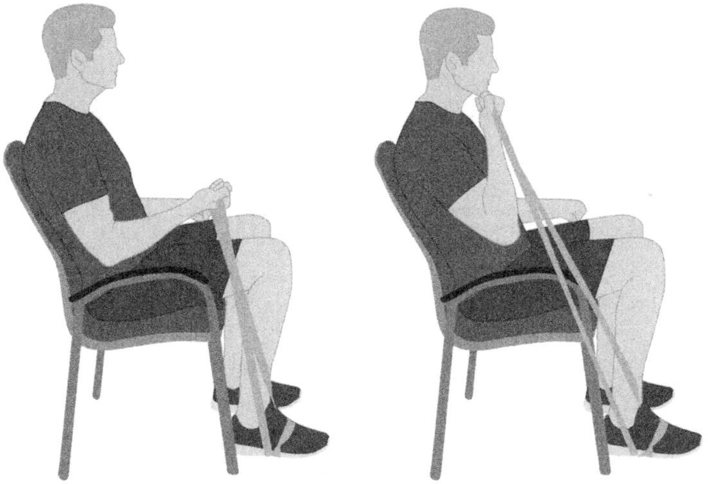

SCAN FOR VIDEO

Chair Exercise #30 Seated Toe Taps

Mobility Rating: **Low**

Muscles Worked: Calves

How to Perform:

1. Sit on the edge of a chair with your feet flat on the floor
2. Keeping your heels on the floor, raise your toes off the floor as high as you can
3. Lower them back down to the starting position

Tips: This is a great exercise for ankle mobility and strength, a key component of balance. The exercise is basically the opposite of the calf raise exercise. Raising your toes instead of your heels.

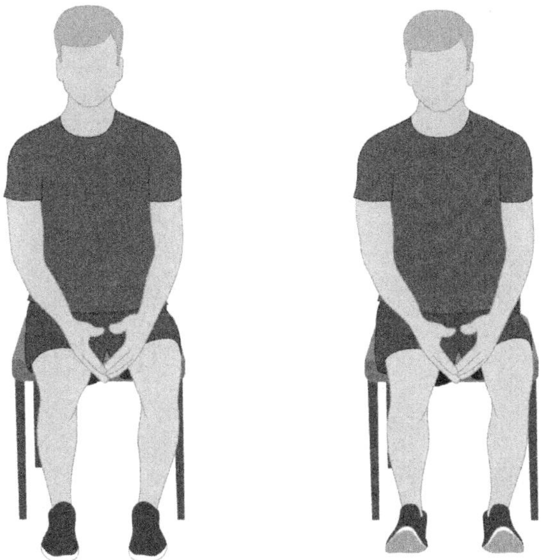

SCAN FOR VIDEO

Chair Exercise Workouts

Exercise Videos

It is often beneficial and easier to see an exercise being performed rather than following written instructions. Which is why, each exercise in this book has a QR code that links to it's video clip.

While all the exercises included in each workout routine below can be accessed individually by scanning their respective QR codes, **if you wish to see all the exercises included in a workout in a single video**, avoiding the necessity of scanning each exercise's QR code one at a time, become part of our community by scanning this QR code.

Low Mobility Chair Workout (*no equipment*)

This workout is perfect if you have low mobility and don't have any equipment other than a sturdy chair to work with. It would be a good idea to purchase some resistance bands (my preference) and/or dumbbells, as these can help you to improve your balance faster. But starting off with this low-mobility chair workout is much better than waiting for new equipment.

Exercise List

- Box Squat (exercise #1)
- Seated Leg Extension (exercise #6)
- Seated Calf Raises (exercise #11)
- Seated Hamstring Curls (exercise #13)
- Standing Hip Extension (exercise #15)
- Single Leg Stand – Knee Forward (exercise #17)
- Single Leg Stand – Heel Back (exercise #18)
- Lateral Lunges (exercise #22)
- Sit and Reach (exercise #26)
- Seated Toe Taps (exercise #30)

Don't forget to add in the low-mobility warm-up (Home) that we looked at earlier. Here is the workout program. Perform this in full, then either workout 1 or 2:

Low-Mobility Warm-up (home)

Exercise	Sets	Reps	Rest Between Sets
Neck Warm Up	1	6	n/a
Shoulder Shrugs	1	5	n/a
Shoulder Rolls	1	5	n/a
Arm Circles	1	10	n/a
High Knees	1 (each leg)	5-10	30 seconds
Reverse Knees	1 (each leg)	5-10	30 seconds
Calf Raises	1	10	n/a

Low Mobility Chair Workout (*no equipment*) - Workout #1

Exercise	Sets	Reps	Rest	Exercise Number
Box Squats	3	10	60-90 seconds	#1
Seated Leg Extension	2 (each leg)	10	30-60 seconds	#6
Seated Hamstring Curls	3	10	30-60 seconds	#13
Seated Calf Raises	3	10	30-60 seconds	#11
Seated Toe Taps	3	10	30-60 seconds	#30

Low Mobility Chair Workout (*no equipment*) - Workout #2

Exercise	Sets	Reps	Rest	Exercise Number
Box Squats	3	10	60-90 seconds	#1
Standing Hip Extension	2 (each leg)	10	30-60 seconds	#15
Single Leg Stand Knee Forward	2 (each leg)	10	30-60 seconds	#17
Single Leg Stand Heel Back	2 (each leg)	10	30-60 seconds	#18
Lateral Lunges	2 (each leg)	10	30-60 seconds	#22
Sit and Reach	2 (each leg)	10	30-60 seconds	#26

You can perform these workouts four times per week on rotation. So a week could look like this:

- **Monday**: Warm up followed by workout #1
- **Tuesday**: Warm up followed by workout #2
- **Wednesday**: Rest
- **Thursday**: Warm up followed by workout #1
- **Friday**: Warm up followed by workout #2
- **Saturday**: Rest
- **Sunday**: Rest

Low Mobility Chair Workout (*equipment*)

This workout is a combination of no-equipment and equipment-based exercises. It isn't necessarily more challenging than the no-equipment workout, but it has the potential to be. It offers more variety, and there are more upper-body exercises available. You will need ankle weights, dumbbells, and resistance bands for this workout.

If any of the weighted exercises in these workouts is too difficult, then just revert to the non-weighted versions.

Exercise List

- Box Squat (exercise #1)
- Seated Leg Extension (exercise #6)
- Seated Leg Extension with ankle weights (exercise #7)
- Seated Hamstring Curls (exercise #13)
- Seated Hamstring Curls with Resistance Band (exercise #14)
- Standing Hip Extension (exercise #15)

- Standing Hip Extension with Ankle Weights (exercise #16)
- Single Leg Stand – Knee Forward (exercise #17)
- Single Leg Stand – Heel Back (exercise #18)
- Lateral Lunges (exercise #22)
- Sit and Reach (exercise #26)
- Seated Resistance Band Bicep Curl (exercise #29)
- Seated Toe Taps (exercise #30)

Low-Mobility Warm-Up (home)

Exercise	Sets	Reps	Rest Between Sets
Neck Warm Up	1	6	n/a
Shoulder Shrugs	1	5	n/a
Shoulder Rolls	1	5	n/a
Arm Circles	1	10	n/a
High Knees	1 (each leg)	5-10	30 seconds
Reverse Knees	1 (each leg)	5-10	30 seconds
Calf Raises	1	10	n/a

Low Mobility Chair Workout (*equipment*) - Workout #3

Exercise	Sets	Reps	Rest	Exercise Number
Box Squats	3	10	60-90 seconds	#1
Seated Leg Extension w/ ankle weights	2 (each leg)	10	60 seconds	#7

Exercise	Sets	Reps	Rest	Exercise Number
Seated Hamstring Curls w/ resistance bands	3	10	30-60 seconds	#14
Seated Calf Raises	3	10	30-60 seconds	#13
Seated Resistance Band Bicep Curls	3	10	30-60 seconds	#29
Seated Toe Taps	3	10	30-60 seconds	#30

Low Mobility Chair Workout (*equipment*) - Workout #4

Exercise	Sets	Reps	Rest	Exercise Number
Box Squats	3	10	60-90 seconds	#1
Standing Hip Extension w/ ankle weights	2 (each leg)	10	30-60 seconds	#16
Single Leg Stand Knee Forward	2 (each leg)	10	30-60 seconds	#17
Single Leg Stand Heel Back	2 (each leg)	10	30-60 seconds	#18
Lateral Lunges	2 (each leg)	10	30-60 seconds	#22

Exercise	Sets	Reps	Rest	Exercise Number
Seated Resistance Band Bicep Curls	3	10	30-60 seconds	#29
Sit and Reach	2 (each leg)	10	30-60 seconds	#26

You can perform these workouts four times per week on rotation. So a week could look like this:

- **Monday**: Warm up followed by workout #3
- **Tuesday**: Warm up followed by workout #4
- **Wednesday**: Rest
- **Thursday**: Warm up followed by workout #3
- **Friday**: Warm up followed by workout #4
- **Saturday**: Rest
- **Sunday**: Rest

Medium Mobility Chair Workout (*no equipment*)

A medium mobility chair workout with no equipment allows you to perform a great upper and lower body workout that will improve your balance over time. If you have the mobility, but you find the workouts too difficult, then go back to low-mobility chair workouts instead until your strength and fitness improve

Our medium-mobility workouts will use both low and medium-mobility exercises, allowing greater variety and more interesting workouts.

Exercise List

- Box Squat (exercise #1)
- Box Squat with Hands Behind or Raised Above Head (exercise #2)
- Seated Leg Extension (exercise #6)
- Seated Leg Extension with Abduction (exercise #9)
- Seated Calf Raises (exercise #11)
- Seated Hamstring Curls (exercise #13)
- Standing Hip Extension (exercise #15)
- Single Leg Stand – Knee Forward (exercise #17)

- Single Leg Stand – Heel Back (exercise #18)
- Leg Swings - Forward & Back (exercise #19)
- Leg Swings – Side to Side (exercise #20)
- Double Leg Lift {exercise #21)
- Lateral Lunges (exercise #22)
- Sit and Reach (exercise #26)
- Sumo Box Squat (exercise #29)
- Seated Toe Taps (exercise #30)

Don't forget to start your sessions with a **medium-mobility home warm-up**:

Exercise	Sets	Reps	Rest Between Sets
Arm Circles	1 (each direction)	6	30 seconds
High Knees	1 (each leg)	5-10	30 seconds
Reverse Knees	1 (each leg)	5-10	30 seconds
Stair Climbing	1	30-60 seconds	n/a

Medium Mobility Chair Workout (*no equipment*) - Workout #5

Exercise	Sets	Reps	Rest	Exercise Number
Box Squats with Hands Behind or Raised Above Head	3	10	60-90 seconds	#2
Seated Leg Extension	2 (each leg)	10	30-60 seconds	#6

Exercise	Sets	Reps	Rest	Exercise Number
Single Leg Stand Knee Forward	2 (each leg)	10	30-60 seconds	#17
Single Leg Stand Heel Back	2 (each leg)	10	30-60 seconds	#18
Sit and Reach	2 (each leg)	10	30-60 seconds	#26
Seated Calf Raises	3	10	30-60 seconds	#11
Double Leg Lift	2	5	60-90 seconds	#21

Medium Mobility Chair Workout (*no equipment*) - Workout #6

Exercise	Sets	Reps	Rest	Exercise Number
Box Squats	3	10	60-90 seconds	#1
Seated Leg Extension w/ abduction	2 (each leg)	10	30-60 seconds	#9
Leg Swings – Forward Back	2 (each leg)	10	30-60 seconds	#19
Leg Swings – Side to Side	2 (each leg)	10	30-60 seconds	#20
Sit and Reach	2 (each leg)	10	30-60 seconds	#26
Seated Toe Taps	3	10	30-60 seconds	#30
Double Leg Lift	2	5	60-90 seconds	#21

Medium Mobility Chair Workout (*no equipment*) - Workout #7

Exercise	Sets	Reps	Rest	Exercise Number
Sumo Box Squats	3	10	60-90 seconds	#29
Lateral Lunges	2 (each leg)	10	30-60 seconds	#22
Seated Hamstring Curls	3	10	30-60 seconds	#13
Standing Hip Extension	2 (each leg)	10	30-60 seconds	#15
Seated Calf Raises	3	10	30-60 seconds	#11
Seated Toe Taps	3	10	30-60 seconds	#30
Double Leg Lift	2	5	60-90 seconds	#21

You can perform this workout 3, 4, 5, or 6 times per week. Here is a sample of what a six-time-per-week workout program would look like:

- **Monday**: Warm up followed by workout #5
- **Tuesday**: Warm up followed by workout #6
- **Wednesday**: Warm up followed by workout #7
- **Thursday**: Rest
- **Friday**: Warm up followed by workout #5
- **Saturday**: Warm up followed by workout #6
- **Sunday**: Warm up followed by workout #7

Medium Mobility Chair Workout (*equipment*)

This workout will combine both low and medium-mobility exercises that either use equipment or not. This workout will require ankle weights, resistance bands, and dumbbells. If you find any of the equipment-requiring exercises too difficult, replace them with their non-equipment counterparts. Or go back to the non-equipment workout above.

Exercise List

- Box Squat with Hands Behind or Raised Above Head (exercise #2)
- Box Squat with Dumbbell (exercise #3)
- Seated Leg Extension (exercise #6)
- Seated Leg Extension with Resistance Band (exercise #8)
- Seated Leg Extension with Abduction (exercise #9)
- Seated Calf Raises with Dumbbells (exercise #12)
- Seated Hamstring Curls (exercise #13)
- Seated Hamstring Curls with Resistance Band (exercise #14)
- Standing Hip Extension (exercise #15)

- Standing Hip Extension with Ankle Weights (exercise #16)
- Single Leg Stand – Knee Forward (exercise #17)
- Double Leg Lift {exercise #21)
- Lateral Lunges (exercise #22)
- Sit and Reach (exercise #26)
- Seated Elbow to Knee (exercise #27)
- Sumo Box Squat (exercise #29)
- Seated Toe Taps (exercise #30)

Medium-mobility home warm-up for you to follow:

Exercise	Sets	Reps	Rest Between Sets
Arm Circles	1 (each direction)	6	30 seconds
High Knees	1 (each leg)	5-10	30 seconds
Reverse Knees	1 (each leg)	5-10	30 seconds
Stair Climbing	1	30-60 seconds	n/a

Medium Mobility Chair Workout (*equipment*) - Workout #8

Exercise	Sets	Reps	Rest	Exercise Number
Box Squats with Dumbbell	3	10	60-90 seconds	#3
Seated Leg Extension w/ resistance band	2 (each leg)	10	30-60 seconds	#8

Exercise	Sets	Reps	Rest	Exercise Number
Single Leg Stand Knee Forward	2 (each leg)	10	30-60 seconds	#17
Single Leg Stand Heel Back	2 (each leg)	10	30-60 seconds	#18
Seated Hamstring Curls w/ resistance band	2 (each leg)	10	30-60 seconds	#14
Seated Calf Raises w/ dumbbells	3	10	30-60 seconds	#12
Double Leg Lift	2	5	60-90 seconds	#21

Medium Mobility Chair Workout (*equipment*) - Workout #9

Exercise	Sets	Reps	Rest	Exercise Number
Box Squats with Hands Behind or Raised Above Head	3	10	60-90 seconds	#2
Seated Leg Extension w/ abduction	2 (each leg)	10	30-60 seconds	#9
Seated Hamstring Curls	2 (each leg)	10	30-60 seconds	#13
Standing Hip Extension	2 (each leg)	10	30-60 seconds	#15

Exercise	Sets	Reps	Rest	Exercise Number
Sit and Reach	2 (each leg)	10	30-60 seconds	#26
Seated Toe Taps	3	10	30-60 seconds	#30
Double Leg Lift	2	5	60-90 seconds	#21

Medium Mobility Chair Workout (*equipment*) - Workout #10

Exercise	Sets	Reps	Rest	Exercise Number
Sumo Box Squats	3	10	60-90 seconds	#29
Lateral Lunges	2 (each leg)	10	30-60 seconds	#22
Seated Hamstring Curls w/ resistance band	3	10	30-60 seconds	#14
Standing Hip Extension w/ ankle weights	2 (each leg)	10	30-60 seconds	#16
Seated Calf Raises w/ dumbbells	3	10	30-60 seconds	#12
Seated Toe Taps	3	10	30-60 seconds	#27
Double Leg Lift	2	5	60-90 seconds	#21

You can perform this workout 3, 4, 5, or 6 times per week. Here is a sample of what a six-time-per-week workout program would look like:

- **Monday**: Warm up followed by workout #8
- **Tuesday**: Warm up followed by workout #9
- **Wednesday**: Warm up followed by workout #10
- **Thursday**: Rest
- **Friday**: Warm up followed by workout #8
- **Saturday**: Warm up followed by workout #9
- **Sunday**: Warm up followed by workout #10

High Mobility Chair Workout (*no equipment*)

A high-mobility workout is designed for people with no mobility issues. However, because many of the exercises are more challenging, even someone with very high mobility may struggle from a strength and fitness point of view. If you feel that this may be the case, then try the medium or even low-mobility workouts first.

Exercise List

- Seated Leg Extension (exercise #6)
- Seated Leg Extension with Abduction (exercise #9)
- Seated Calf Raises (exercise #11)
- Seated Hamstring Curls (exercise #13)
- Standing Hip Extension (exercise #15)
- Single Leg Stand – Knee Forward (exercise #17)
- Single Leg Stand – Heel Back (exercise #18)
- Leg Swings - Forward & Back (exercise #19)
- Leg Swings – Side to Side (exercise #20)
- Double Leg Lift {exercise #21)
- Lateral Lunges (exercise #22)
- Squats while Holding Chair (exercise #23)

- Sumo Squats while Holding Chair (exercise #24)
- Sit and Reach (exercise #26)
- Seated Elbow to Knee (exercise #27)
- Sumo Box Squat (exercise #28)
- Seated Toe Taps (exercise #30)

*Very difficult exercise. Add it to your training if you feel capable. But approach with caution.

Here is the high-mobility home warm-up. You should start each workout with this:

Exercise	Sets	Reps	Rest Between Sets
Jogging on the Spot	1	30-60 seconds	n/a
Mountain Climbers	1	40-60 seconds	n/a
Lateral Lunges	1 (each leg)	10	30 seconds
Bodyweight Squats	2	10	30 seconds

High Mobility Chair Workout (*no equipment*) - Workout #11

Exercise	Sets	Reps	Rest	Exercise Number
Squats while Holding Chair	3	10	60-90 seconds	#23
Seated Leg Extension	2 (each leg)	10	30-60 seconds	#6
Single Leg Stand Knee Forward	2 (each leg)	10	30-60 seconds	#17

Exercise	Sets	Reps	Rest	Exercise Number
Single Leg Stand Heel Back	2 (each leg)	10	30-60 seconds	#18
Sit and Reach	2 (each leg)	10	30-60 seconds	#26
Seated Calf Raises	3	10	30-60 seconds	#11
Seated Elbow to Knee	3	10	60-90 seconds	#27

High Mobility Chair Workout (*no equipment*) - Workout #12

Exercise	Sets	Reps	Rest	Exercise Number
Sumo Squats while Holding Chair	3	10	60-90 seconds	#24
Seated Leg Extension w/ abduction	2 (each leg)	10	30-60 seconds	#9
Leg Swings – Forward Back	2 (each leg)	10	30-60 seconds	#19
Leg Swings – Side to Side	2 (each leg)	10	30-60 seconds	#20
Seated Hamstring Curls	2 (each leg)	10	30-60 seconds	#13
Seated Toe Taps	3	10	30-60 seconds	#30
Double Leg Lift	2	5	60-90 seconds	#21

High Mobility Chair Workout (*no equipment*) - Workout #13

Exercise	Sets	Reps	Rest	Exercise Number
Sumo Box Squats	3	10	60-90 seconds	#28
Lateral Lunges	2 (each leg)	10	30-60 seconds	#22
Squats while Holding Chair	3	10	30-60 seconds	#23
Standing Hip Extension	2 (each leg)	10	30-60 seconds	#15
Seated Calf Raises	3	10	30-60 seconds	#11
Seated Toe Taps	3	10	30-60 seconds	#30
Seated Elbow to Knee	3	10	60-90 seconds	#27

You can perform this workout 3, 4, 5, or 6 times per week. Here is a sample of what a six-time-per-week workout program would look like:

- **Monday**: Warm up followed by workout #11
- **Tuesday**: Warm up followed by workout #12
- **Wednesday**: Warm up followed by workout #13
- **Thursday**: Rest
- **Friday**: Warm up followed by workout #11
- **Saturday**: Warm up followed by workout #12
- **Sunday**: Warm up followed by workout #13

High Mobility Chair Workout (*equipment*)

This is the final chair workout, and it is designed for someone with high levels of mobility and access to dumbbells, resistance bands, and ankle weights. If you don't have this equipment or you feel that you may be lacking the strength and cardiovascular fitness to complete the workout, then drop down to a lower-mobility workout instead.

Exercise List

- Box Squat with Dumbbell (exercise #3)
- Box Squat into Shoulder Press – Dumbbells (exercise #4) *
- Seated Leg Extension (exercise #6)
- Seated Leg Extension with Ankle Weights (exercise #7) *
- Seated Leg Extension with Resistance Band (exercise #8)
- Seated Leg Extension with Abduction - Ankle Weights (exercise #10)
- Seated Calf Raises (exercise #11)
- Seated Calf Raises with Dumbbells (exercise #12)

- Single Leg Stand – Knee Forward (exercise #17)
- Single Leg Stand – Heel Back (exercise #18)
- Leg Swings - Forward & Back (exercise #19)
- Double Leg Lift {exercise #21)
- Squats while Holding Chair (exercise #23)
- Sumo Squats while Holding Chair (exercise #24)
- Single-Leg Romanian Deadlift (exercise #25) *
- Sit and Reach (exercise #26)
- Seated Resistance Band Bicep Curl (exercise #29) *

*Very difficult exercise. Add it to your training if you feel capable. But approach with caution.

Start each of your workouts with the high-mobility home warm-up so that you are physically and mentally prepared to begin.

Exercise	**Sets**	**Reps**	**Rest Between Sets**
Jogging on the Spot	1	30-60 seconds	n/a
Mountain Climbers	1	40-60 seconds	n/a
Lateral Lunges	1 (each leg)	10	30 seconds
Bodyweight Squats	2	10	30 seconds

As there are so many exercises to choose from, we're going to provide a five-day workout. Each workout is a full-body workout, so if five is too much for you, then you can follow just three or four per week.

High Mobility Chair Workout (*equipment*) - Workout #14

Exercise	Sets	Reps	Rest	Exercise Number
Squats while Holding Chair	3	10	60-90 seconds	#23
Seated Leg Extension w/ ankle weights	2 (each leg)	10	30-60 seconds	#7
Single Leg Stand Knee Forward	2 (each leg)	10	30-60 seconds	#17
Single Leg Romanian Deadlift	2 (each leg)	10	30-60 seconds	#25
Seated Resistance Band Bicep Curl	3	10	30-60 seconds	#29
Seated Calf Raises	3	10	30-60 seconds	#11
Seated Elbow to Knee	3	10	60-90 seconds	#26

High Mobility Chair Workout (*equipment*) - Workout #15

Exercise	Sets	Reps	Rest	Exercise Number
Box Squat into Shoulder Press	3	10	60-90 seconds	#4
Seated Leg Extension w/ resistance band	2 (each leg)	10	30-60 seconds	#8
Leg Swings - Forward & Back	2 (each leg)	10	30-60 seconds	#19
Single Leg Stand Heel Back	2 (each leg)	10	30-60 seconds	#18
Sit and Reach	2 (each leg)	10	30-60 seconds	#26
Seated Calf Raises w/ dumbbells	3	10	30-60 seconds	#12
Double Leg Lift	2	5	60-90 seconds	#21

High Mobility Chair Workout (*equipment*) - Workout #16

Exercise	Sets	Reps	Rest	Exercise Number
Sumo Squats while Holding Chair	3	10	60-90 seconds	#24
Seated Leg Extension	2 (each leg)	10	30-60 seconds	#6

Exercise	Sets	Reps	Rest	Exercise Number
Single Leg Stand Knee Forward	2 (each leg)	10	30-60 seconds	#17
Single Leg Romanian Deadlift	2 (each leg)	10	30-60 seconds	#25
Seated Resistance Band Bicep Curl	3	10	30-60 seconds	#29
Seated Calf Raises	3	10	30-60 seconds	#11
Seated Elbow to Knee	3	10	60-90 seconds	#26

High Mobility Chair Workout (*equipment*) - Workout #17

Exercise	Sets	Reps	Rest	Exercise Number
Box Squat with Dumbbell	3	10	60-90 seconds	#3
Seated Leg Extension w/ Abduction – Ankle Weights	2 (each leg)	10	30-60 seconds	#10
Leg Swings - Forward & Back	2 (each leg)	10	30-60 seconds	#19
Single Leg Stand Heel Back	2 (each leg)	10	30-60 seconds	#18

Exercise	Sets	Reps	Rest	Exercise Number
Seated Resistance Band Bicep Curl	3	10	30-60 seconds	#29
Seated Calf Raises w/ dumbbells	3	10	30-60 seconds	#12
Double Leg Lift	2	5	60-90 seconds	#21

High Mobility Chair Workout (*equipment*) - Workout #18

Exercise	Sets	Reps	Rest	Exercise Number
Box Squat into Shoulder Press	3	10	60-90 seconds	#4
Seated Leg Extension w/ ankle weights	2 (each leg)	10	30-60 seconds	#7
Single Leg Stand Knee Forward	2 (each leg)	10	30-60 seconds	#17
Single Leg Romanian Deadlift	2 (each leg)	10	30-60 seconds	#25
Seated Resistance Band Bicep Curl	3	10	30-60 seconds	#29
Seated Calf Raises	3	10	30-60 seconds	#11
Seated Elbow to Knee	3	10	60-90 seconds	#26

This workout is best followed five times per week. But you can follow it three, four, five, or even six times and still get excellent results.

- **Monday**: Warm up followed by workout #14
- **Tuesday**: Warm up followed by workout #15
- **Wednesday**: Warm up followed by workout #16
- **Thursday**: Rest
- **Friday**: Warm up followed by workout #17
- **Saturday**: Warm up followed by workout #18
- **Sunday**: Rest

CHAPTER 6

Bodyweight Exercises

"A year from now you will wish you had started today."

Karen Lamb

Chapter Five looked at several chair-based exercises that were perfect for increasing your balance and mobility. There were workouts that could help people of all fitness and mobility levels. All you needed was a chair (or some basic equipment such as dumbbells and resistance bands)

In this chapter, we are going to be looking at bodyweight exercises. Again, these are exercises that require no equipment whatsoever. Just a secure surface and some space to perform each exercise in.

The chapter will contain 20 bodyweight exercises, split between workouts for low-mobility, medium-mobility, and high-mobility. But you can also combine some bodyweight exercises with your chair workouts to create more varied training sessions.

We will use the same warm-ups as in Chapter Five, and unlike Chapter Five, we will not create a home, gym, or outdoor workout. Quite simply because bodyweight exercises do not use equipment and will therefore stay the same whatever location you are training in.

Many of the exercises on this list will be for medium or high-mobility people. This is because a lot of balance and muscular endurance is required to perform the vast majority of bodyweight exercises. Those with limited mobility or fitness may need to return to Chapter Five's chair exercises. However, you will still get a great workout this way, and you can use them to build the balance and mobility required to perform bodyweight exercises.

20 Bodyweight Exercises

Here are twenty bodyweight exercises for you to learn. Keep an eye out for the mobility rating for each exercise, and only perform them if you are mobile enough to do so. There are more than enough exercises for low-mobility and medium-mobility people to perform. No need to risk injury by trying to force yourself into an exercise your body isn't quite ready for!

Bodyweight Exercise #31 Wall Push-Ups

Mobility Rating: **Low**

Muscles Worked: Pectorals, Triceps, Traps, Deltoids

How to Perform:

1. Stand upright in front of a wall, and place both hands on it, about shoulder-width apart. Your arms should be fully extended
2. Bend your elbows and lean forwards until your chest is almost touching the wall
3. Pause, and then drive your chest backwards to the starting position

Tips: Most people find that having their hands at shoulder height works best, but experiment with placing your hands slightly higher or lower to see if this improves how the exercise feels.

SCAN FOR VIDEO

Bodyweight Exercise #32 Box Push-Ups

Mobility Rating: **Low**

Muscles Worked: Pectorals, Triceps, Traps, Deltoids

How to Perform:

1. Place your hands on the floor, shoulder width apart
2. Place your knees on the floor, and rest your feet on the floor
3. Lower your chest down to the ground by bending your elbows
4. Pause when your chest is almost touching the ground, then rise back up

Tips: You want your elbows to be at a 45-degree angle from your sides rather than a 90-degree angle. This is to prevent your shoulder from hurting.

SCAN FOR VIDEO

Bodyweight Exercise #33
Knee Push-Ups

Mobility Rating: **Medium**

Muscles Worked: Pectorals, Triceps, Traps, Deltoids

How to Perform:

1. Place your hands on the floor, shoulder width apart
2. Place your knees on the floor, and raise your feet in the air
3. Lower your chest down to the ground by bending your elbows
4. Pause when your chest is almost touching the ground, then rise back up

Tips: The further back your knees are, the harder the exercise is. Bring your knees close to your chest if you are finding the exercise too hard.

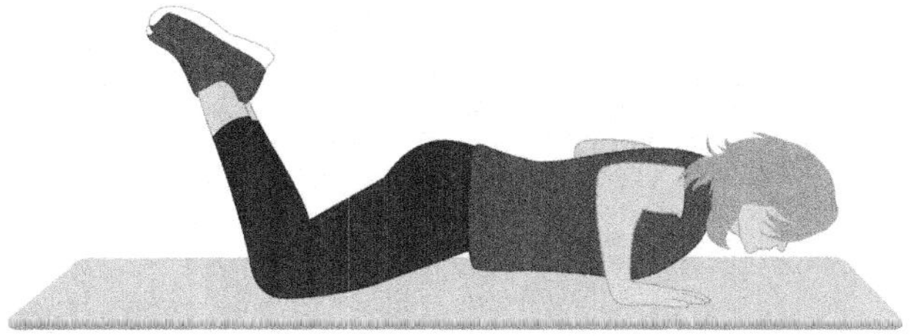

SCAN FOR VIDEO

Bodyweight Exercise #34 Push-Ups

Mobility Rating: **High**

Muscles Worked: Pectorals, Triceps, Traps, Deltoids

How to Perform:

1. Place your hands on the floor, shoulder-width apart
2. Place your feet on the floor, and raise your hips up until there is a straight line from your shoulders down to your heels.
3. Keeping your elbows at a 45-degree angle from your body, lower your chest all the way down until it almost touches the ground.
4. Pause, and then rise back upwards to complete your push-up.

Tips: If the exercise becomes too difficult, you can just lower your knees to the floor and raise your feet in the air. This will make the exercise easier by reducing the amount of your body weight that you are lifting.

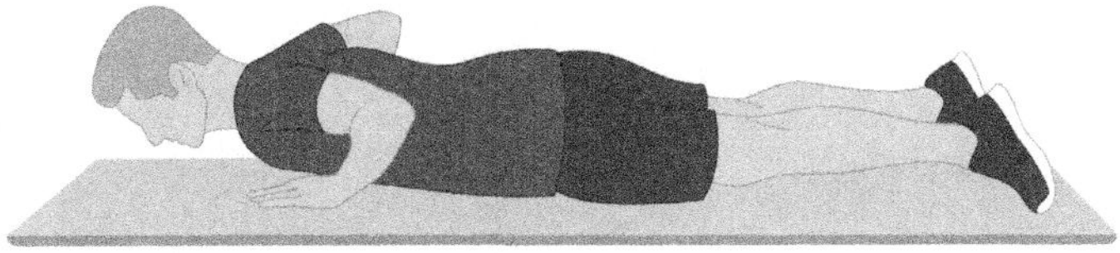

SCAN FOR VIDEO

Bodyweight Exercise #35
Bodyweight Squats

Mobility Rating: **Medium**

Muscles Worked: Glutes, Hamstrings, Quadriceps, Abdominals

How to Perform:

1. Stand upright with your chest pushed out and shoulders pulled back
2. Place your feet shoulder-width apart with toes turned out slightly
3. Ensure that your heels stay in contact with the ground at all times
4. Push your glutes backwards and down as if you were about to sit on a small chair
5. Keep lowering your glutes until your thighs are around parallel to the ground
6. Pause, and then rise back upwards

Tips: The reason most people struggle with squats is a fear of falling down rather than mobility issues. If you have high mobility but find squats difficult to do, then you should consider going back to chair squats and then pausing just before you touch the seat.

SCAN FOR VIDEO

Bodyweight Exercise #36
Bodyweight Sumo Squats

Mobility Rating: **Medium**

Muscles Worked: Glutes, Hamstrings, Quadriceps, Abdominals

How to Perform:

1. Stand upright with your chest pushed out and shoulders pulled back
2. Place your feet wider shoulder-width apart with toes turned out
3. Ensure that your heels stay in contact with the ground at all times
4. Push your glutes backwards and down as if you were about to sit on a small chair
5. Keep lowering your glutes until your thighs are around parallel to the ground
6. Pause, and then rise back upwards

Tips: Because of the very wide stance of sumo squats, you may find that you can't squat down as low as you can during a regular squat.

SCAN FOR VIDEO

Bodyweight Exercise #37 Rock the Boat

Mobility Rating: **Low**

Muscles Worked: Glutes, abdominals, calves, hamstrings, quadriceps

---

How to Perform:

1. Stand upright with feet shoulder-width apart, chest pushed out and shoulders pulled back
2. Transfer your weight onto your right leg, and then raise your left leg in the air
3. Using your arms to balance, hold this position for up to 30 seconds
4. Swap legs and repeat

Tips: If you are not confident, then you can perform this exercise near a wall or chair that is within grabbing reach.

SCAN FOR VIDEO

Bodyweight Exercise #38
Marching in Place

Mobility Rating: **Low**

Muscles Worked: Quadriceps, hamstrings, glutes, calves, abdominals

---

How to Perform:

1. Stand upright with feet together
2. Push your chest out and pull your shoulder blades together
3. Raise one knee up in the air until your thigh is parallel to the ground
4. Lower it back down and raise your opposite knee up in the air
5. Continue marching for 30 seconds

Tips: This exercise is all about balance and working your cardiovascular system, it is a great way to practice for step ups and lunges.

SCAN FOR VIDEO

Bodyweight Exercise #39 Glute Bridges

Mobility Rating: **Medium**

Muscles Worked: Glutes, Hamstrings, Abdominals

How to Perform:

1. Lie on your back with your knees bent and your feet flat on the ground
2. Keeping your head and shoulders on the floor, raise your hips up off the ground
3. Continue raising your hips until there is a straight line from your knees down to your shoulders
4. Squeeze your glutes hard
5. Lower your hips back down to the floor.

Tips: The wider your feet are when starting, the more the exercise will work your hip flexors. Experiment with having your feet closer and wider apart to find a comfortable and effective position.

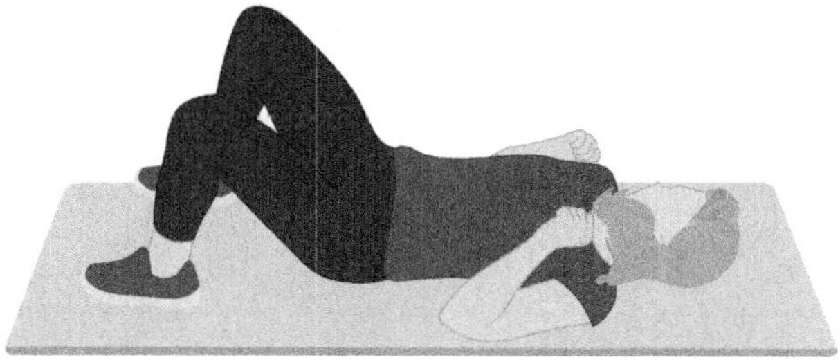

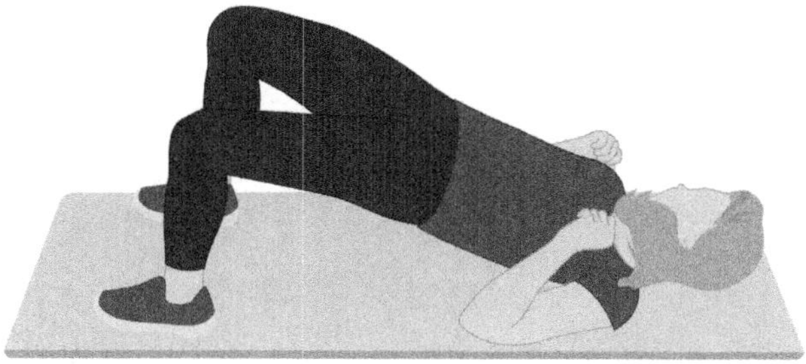

SCAN FOR VIDEO

Bodyweight Exercise #40

Lateral Lunges

Mobility Rating: **Medium**

Muscles Worked: Quadriceps, hamstrings, glutes, adductors, abductors

---

How to Perform:

1. Stand upright with chest out and shoulder blades pulled together. Your feet should be together
2. With your right foot, take a wide step to the right, keeping your left foot in place
3. Bend your right knee while keeping your left leg straight
4. Pause and then return to the starting position

Tips: Try to ensure that your knee doesn't travel over your foot when bending your leg

SCAN FOR VIDEO

Bodyweight Exercise #41
Walking Lunges

Mobility Rating: **High**

Muscles Worked: Glutes, Quadriceps, Abdominals

How to Perform:

1. Stand upright with chest out and shoulder blades pulled together. Your feet should be together
2. Take a large step forward with your left foot, raise your right heel off the floor
3. Drop your right knee towards the floor, pausing just before it touches
4. Your left thigh should now be parallel to the floor
5. Keep your chest upright throughout
6. Pause, and then rise back up and bring your right foot forwards.
7. Repeat the movement with the opposite legs to walk forward

Tips: This exercise can really work your core, as it is hard to balance. You can use your arms to help balance if you are struggling.

SCAN FOR VIDEO

Bodyweight Exercise #42 Side Lying Leg Circles

Mobility Rating: **Low**

Muscles Worked: Quadriceps, hamstrings, glutes, abdominals

How to Perform:

1. Lie on your right side with your body in a nice and straight line
2. Prop your head up with one arm, using your other arm to balance yourself
3. Raise your left leg up in the air, and then start to move it in a small circle
4. Perform the requisite number of reps, and then swap sides and repeat

Tips: Slow the movement down and really concentrate on moving your leg in tight circles. This will provide a proper workout.

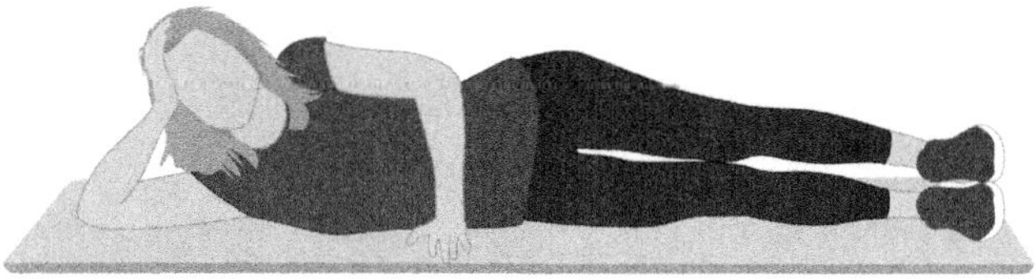

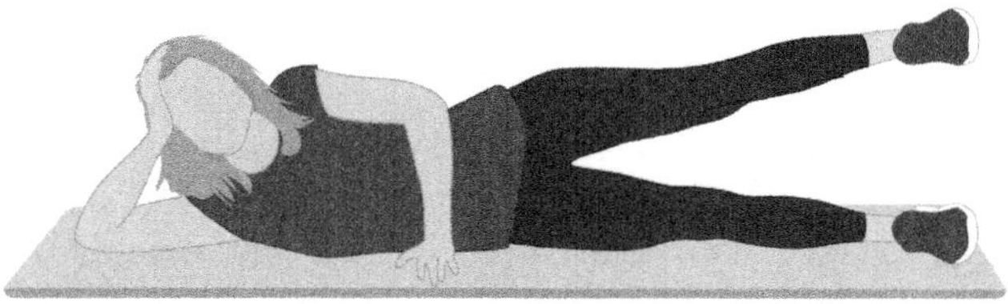

SCAN FOR VIDEO

Bodyweight Exercise #43 Tricep Dip

Mobility Rating: **Medium**

Muscles Worked: Triceps, Deltoids

How to Perform:

1. Sit on the floor with your feet flat on the ground and your hands flat on the ground facing forward
2. Raise your body off the floor so that you are in an M shape with arms fully straight
3. Lower your glutes towards the floor, bending your arms as you do so
4. Pause when you are almost touching the floor, then use your arms to drive yourself back upwards

Tips: You can turn this into a balance exercise by raising one foot slightly off the ground. You can increase the difficulty by placing your hands on a slightly raised surface.

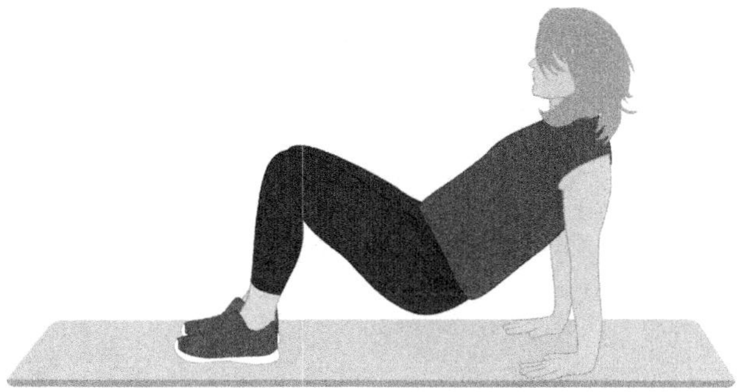

SCAN FOR VIDEO

Bodyweight Exercise #44 Plank (Push-Up Position)

Mobility Rating: **Medium**

Muscles Worked: Abdominals, Deltoids, Glutes, Hamstrings, Triceps

---

How to Perform:

1. Place your hands on the floor, shoulder-width apart
2. Place your feet on the floor, and raise your hips up until there is a straight line from your shoulders down to your heels.
3. Squeeze your abs tight, and squeeze your glutes
4. Hold this position for 30 seconds and then relax

Tips: Often, people hold planks for as long as possible, but this can lead to a weaker contraction of the muscles. Instead, holding planks for a pre-determined time (30 seconds) allows you to hold the position with better form and at a higher intensity. Squeeze as hard as you can for those 30 seconds.

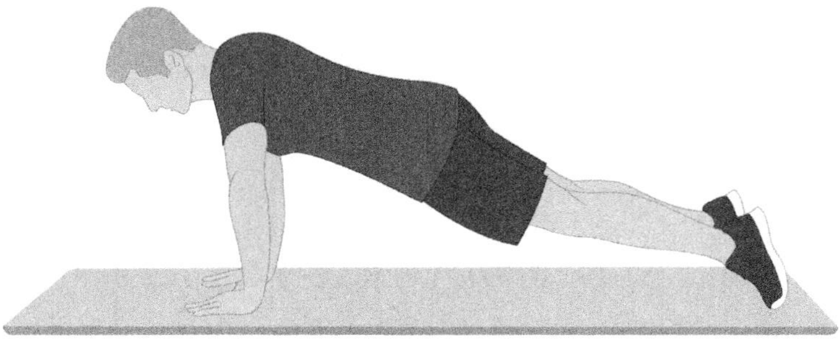

SCAN FOR VIDEO

Bodyweight Exercise #45 Side Plank

Mobility Rating: **Medium**

Muscles Worked: Obliques, abdominals, lower back

How to Perform:

1. Lie on your right side with your legs straight and one foot resting on the other
2. Rest your right forearm on the ground straight out in front of you
3. Raise your right hip off the floor, resting your left hand on your left hip
4. Pause when your body is in a nice straight line
5. Hold for 30 seconds, then relax, swap sides and repeat

Tips: This exercise can place a lot of pressure on your shoulder and forearm, if you find it uncomfortable, you can perform an elevated side plank, which is where your arm is fully extended rather than bent at the elbow.

SCAN FOR VIDEO

Modified Plank

SCAN FOR VIDEO

Bodyweight Exercise #46 Reverse Abdominal Crunches

Mobility Rating: **Medium**

Muscles Worked: Abdominals

How to Perform:

1. Lie on your back with your hands placed under your tailbone
2. Your feet should be flat on the floor and knees bent
3. Raise your feet in the air and bring your knees towards your chest
4. Pause and then return your feet to the floor

Tips: You can make this exercise more difficult by raising your glutes off the floor while bringing your knees towards your chest.

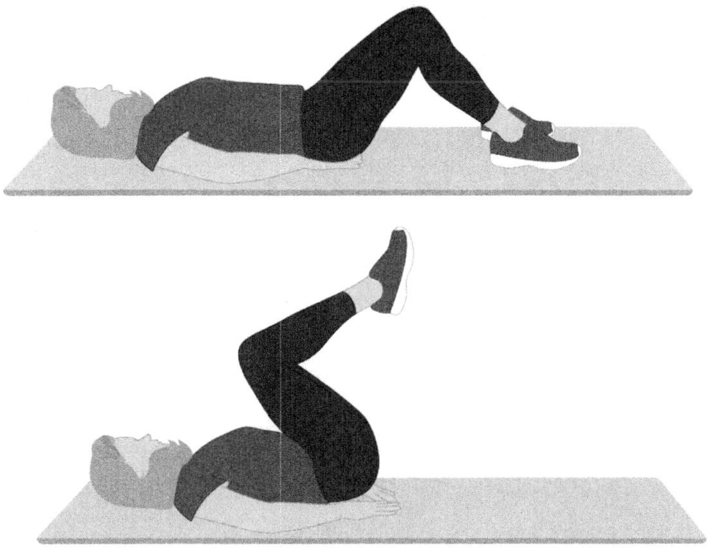

SCAN FOR VIDEO

Bodyweight Exercise #47 Wood Chops

Mobility Rating: **Medium**

Muscles Worked: Abdominals, obliques

How to Perform:

1. Stand upright with feet shoulder-width apart
2. Hold your hands together, resting beside your left hip
3. Swing your arms across your body and upwards as if you were swinging an axe
4. Pause when your arms are raised above your right shoulder
5. Swing back to the starting position

Tips: You can increase the range of motion by bending your knees at the start and end of the exercise.

SCAN FOR VIDEO

Bodyweight Exercise #48 Superman

Mobility Rating: **Medium**

Muscles Worked: Abdominals, lower back

How to Perform:

1. Lie on your front with arms and legs straight
2. Raise your legs and arms up in the air, keeping them straight throughout. Your chest should also rise off the floor
3. Hold for a second or two, then lower your arms, chest, and legs back down

Tips: You can make this easier by raising one arm and the opposing leg at the same time and then swapping both arm and leg for the next rep

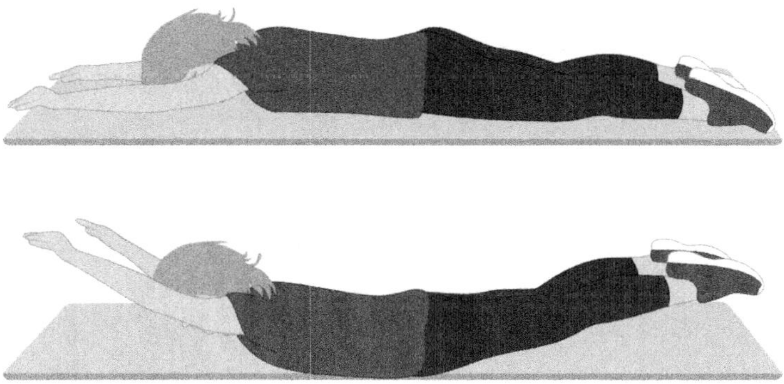

SCAN FOR VIDEO

Bodyweight Exercise #49 Dead Bugs

Mobility Rating: **Medium**

Muscles Worked: Abdominals

How to Perform:

1. Lie on your back with your arms straight up in the air
2. Raise your feet up in the air with knees bent at a 90 degree angle
3. Lower your left arm to the floor (above your head)
4. At the same time, lower your right leg and straighten it
5. Stop both before they touch the ground and return them to the starting position
6. Switch arms and legs and repeat

Tips: Make the exercise easier by performing it with just the arms or the legs lowering to the ground and rising back upwards.

SCAN FOR VIDEO

Bodyweight Exercise #50 Bird Dog Exercise

Mobility Rating: **Medium**

Muscles Worked: Lower back, abdominals

How to Perform:

1. Kneel on the floor and place your hands flat on the ground in front of you
2. Raise your right hand off the ground and extend it out in front of you
3. At the same time, raise your left leg off the floor and push it back behind you
4. Pause when both your arm and your leg are fully extended in the air
5. Now pull arm and leg back in until your elbow touches your knee, then extend both again
6. Repeat for correct number of reps and then swap to the opposite arm and leg

Tips: You can make the exercise into a plank variation by holding the pose when arm and leg are extended for 30 seconds each side.

SCAN FOR VIDEO

Bodyweight Workouts

Exercise Videos

It is often beneficial and easier to see an exercise being performed rather than following written instructions. Which is why, each exercise in this book has a QR code that links to it's video clip.

While all the exercises included in each workout routine below can be accessed individually by scanning their respective QR codes, **if you wish to see all the exercises included in a workout in a single video**, avoiding the necessity of scanning each exercise's QR code one at a time, become part of our community by scanning this QR code.

SCAN FOR VIDEO

Low Mobility Bodyweight Workout

There aren't many low-mobility bodyweight exercises on this list, so we will be combining them with some of the low-mobility chair exercises from the previous chapter. This will ensure that you get a full-body workout that is safe and challenging.

Here are five bodyweight exercises that are suitable for people with low mobility:

Exercise List

- Wall Push-Ups (exercise #31)
- Box Push-Ups (exercise #32)
- Rock the Boat (exercise #37)
- Marching in Place (exercise #38)
- Side Lying Leg Circles (exercise #42)

We will be combining these exercises with the following chair exercises that are also suitable for low-mobility people.

- Box Squat (exercise #1)
- Seated Leg Extension (exercise #6)
- Seated Hamstring Curls (exercise #13)
- Standing Hip Extension (exercise #15)

- Single Leg Stand – Knee Forward (exercise #17)
- Single Leg Stand – Heel Back (exercise #18)
- Sit and Reach (exercise #26)

Start things off with the low-mobility warm-up we looked at earlier:

Exercise	Sets	Reps	Rest Between Sets
Neck Warm Up	1	6	n/a
Shoulder Shrugs	1	5	n/a
Shoulder Rolls	1	5	n/a
Arm Circles	1	10	n/a
High Knees	1 (each leg)	5-10	30 seconds
Reverse Knees	1 (each leg)	5-10	30 seconds
Calf Raises	1	10	n/a

We will create two workouts, you can perform them each week. All you will need is a sturdy chair or an exercise bench.

Low Mobility Bodyweight - Workout #19

Exercise	Sets	Reps	Rest	Exercise Number
Box Squats	3	10	60-90 seconds	#1
Seated Leg Extension	2 (each leg)	10	30-60 seconds	#6
Seated Hamstring Curls	3	10	30-60 seconds	#13

Exercise	Sets	Reps	Rest	Exercise Number
Marching in Place	3	30 second	30-60 seconds	#38
Wall Push-Ups	3	10	30-60 seconds	#31
Side Lying Leg Circles	2 (each leg)	10	30-60 seconds	#42

Low Mobility Bodyweight - Workout #20

Exercise	Sets	Reps	Rest	Exercise Number
Box Squats	3	10	60-90 seconds	#1
Standing Hip Extension	2 (each leg)	10	30-60 seconds	#15
Single Leg Stand Knee Forward	2 (each leg)	10	30-60 seconds	#17
Single Leg Stand Heel Back	2 (each leg)	10	30-60 seconds	#18
Rock the Boat	2 (each leg)	10	30-60 seconds	#37
Box Push-Ups	3	10	30-60 seconds	#32
Sit and Reach	2 (each leg)	10	30-60 seconds	#26

You can perform these workouts four times per week on rotation. So a week could look like this:

- **Monday**: Warm up followed by workout #19
- **Tuesday**: Warm up followed by workout #20
- **Wednesday**: Rest
- **Thursday**: Warm up followed by workout #19
- **Friday**: Warm up followed by workout #20
- **Saturday**: Rest
- **Sunday**: Rest

Medium Mobility Bodyweight Workout

Unlike the low-mobility bodyweight workout, the medium version will not need to rely on chair exercises to fill out the program. That's because there are more than enough low and medium mobility exercises for you to perform.

Exercise List

- Wall Push-Ups (exercise #31)
- Box Push-Ups (exercise #32)
- Knee Push-Ups (exercise #33)
- Bodyweight Squats (exercise #35)
- Bodyweight Sumo Squats (exercise #36)
- Rock the Boat (exercise #37)
- Marching in Place (exercise #38)
- Glute Bridges (exercise #39)
- Lateral Lunges (exercise #40)
- Tricep Dips (exercise #43)
- Plank (exercise #44)
- Reverse Abdominal Crunches (exercise #46)
- Wood Chops (exercise #47)
- Superman (exercise #48)

For your warm-up, you can either follow the low-mobility warm-up from earlier or you can follow the medium-mobility warm-up, which looks like this:

Exercise	Sets	Reps	Rest Between Sets
Brisk Walk/Jog	1	60-150 seconds	n/a
Arm Circles	1 (each direction)	6	30 seconds
High Knees	1 (each leg)	5-10	30 seconds
Reverse Knees	1 (each leg)	5-10	30 seconds

We will create four different workouts for this medium-mobility bodyweight program. You can perform each one during the week, with three rest days.

Medium Mobility Bodyweight - Workout #21

Exercise	Sets	Reps	Rest	Exercise Number
Bodyweight Squats	3	10	60-90 seconds	#35
Glute Bridges	3	10	60-90 seconds	#39
Marching in Place	3	30 second	60-90 seconds	#38
Box Push Ups	3	15	60-90 seconds	#32
Plank	3	30 second	60-90 seconds	#44
Superman	3	10	60-90 seconds	#48

Medium Mobility Bodyweight - Workout #22

Exercise	Sets	Reps	Rest	Exercise Number
Bodyweight Sumo Squats	3	10	60-90 seconds	#36
Glute Bridges	3	10	60-90 seconds	#39
Lateral Lunges	2 (each leg)	10	60-90 seconds	#40
Knee Push-Ups	3	10	60-90 seconds	#33
Tricep Dips	3	10	60-90 seconds	#43
Wood Chops	2 (each arm)	10	60-90 seconds	#47

Medium Mobility Bodyweight - Workout #23

Exercise	Sets	Reps	Rest	Exercise Number
Bodyweight Squats	3	10	60-90 seconds	#35
Glute Bridges	3	10	60-90 seconds	#39
Rock the Boat	2 (each leg)	30 second	60-90 seconds	#37
Wall Push-Ups	3	15	60-90 seconds	#31
Tricep Dips	3	10	60-90 seconds	#43
Reverse Abdominal Crunches	3	10	60-90 seconds	#46

Medium Mobility Bodyweight - Workout #24

Exercise	Sets	Reps	Rest	Exercise Number
Bodyweight Sumo Squats	3	10	60-90 seconds	#36
Glute Bridges	3	10	60-90 seconds	#39
Lateral Lunges	2 (each leg)	10	60-90 seconds	#40
Box Push Ups	3	15	60-90 seconds	#32
Tricep Dips	3	10	60-90 seconds	#43
Wood Chops	2 (each arm)	10	60-90 seconds	#47

You can perform these workouts four times per week on rotation. So a week could look like this:

- **Monday**: Warm up followed by workout #21
- **Tuesday**: Warm up followed by workout #22
- **Wednesday**: Rest
- **Thursday**: Warm up followed by workout #23
- **Friday**: Warm up followed by workout #24
- **Saturday**: Rest
- **Sunday**: Rest

High Mobility Workout

This is the toughest workout of the three. Remember, if you are highly mobile, but you don't feel fit enough to complete these sessions, then you can perform the medium or even low-mobility workouts and build your fitness.

Exercise List

- Push-Ups (exercise #34)
- Bodyweight Squats (exercise #35)
- Bodyweight Sumo Squats (exercise #36)
- Glute Bridges (exercise #39)
- Walking Lunges (exercise #41)
- Tricep Dips (exercise #43)
- Plank (exercise #44)
- Reverse Abdominal Crunches (exercise #46)
- Wood Chops (exercise #47)
- Superman (exercise #48)

We will start off with the high-mobility warm-up, but feel free to use the low or medium-mobility warm-ups if you prefer them.

Exercise	Sets	Reps	Rest Between Sets
Gentle Burpees	1	10	n/a
Sumo Squats	1	10	n/a
Lateral Lunges	1 (each leg)	10	30 seconds
Mountain Climbers	1	30-40 seconds	n/a
Body Get Ups	2	5	30 seconds

There are only two new exercises in this program (push-ups and walking lunges), so the training program is going to be almost identical to the medium-mobility program, but with these two exercises taking prominence.

The idea is to build up the number of push-ups you can do over time, so they will be used instead of wall push-ups, box push-ups, and kneeling push-ups. If you can't manage to perform a full set of push-ups, do as many as you can, then drop down to kneeling push-ups to finish the set.

High Mobility Workout - Workout #25

Exercise	Sets	Reps	Rest	Exercise Number
Bodyweight Squats	3	10	60-90 seconds	#35
Glute Bridges	3	10	60-90 seconds	#39
Walking Lunges	4	20	60-90 seconds	#41
Push-Ups	3	5-10	90 seconds	#34
Plank	3	30 second	60-90 seconds	#44
Superman	3	10	60-90 seconds	#48

High Mobility Workout - Workout #26

Exercise	Sets	Reps	Rest	Exercise Number
Bodyweight Sumo Squats	3	10	60-90 seconds	#36
Glute Bridges	3	10	60-90 seconds	#39
Walking Lunges	4	20	60-90 seconds	#41
Push-Ups	3	5-10	90 seconds	#34
Tricep Dips	3	10	60-90 seconds	#43
Wood Chops	2 (each arm)	10	60-90 seconds	#47

High Mobility Workout - Workout #27

Exercise	Sets	Reps	Rest	Exercise Number
Bodyweight Squats	3	10	60-90 seconds	#35
Glute Bridges	3	10	60-90 seconds	#39
Walking Lunges	4	20	60-90 seconds	#41
Push-Ups	3	5-10	90 seconds	#34
Tricep Dips	3	10	60-90 seconds	#43
Reverse Abdominal Crunches	3	10	60-90 seconds	#46

High Mobility Workout - Workout #28

Exercise	Sets	Reps	Rest	Exercise Number
Bodyweight Sumo Squats	3	10	60-90 seconds	#36
Glute Bridges	3	10	60-90 seconds	#39
Walking Lunges	4	20	60-90 seconds	#41
Push-Ups	3	5-10	90 seconds	#34
Tricep Dips	3	10	60-90 seconds	#43
Wood Chops	2 (each arm)	10	60-90 seconds	#47

You can perform these workouts four times per week on rotation. So a week could look like this:

- **Monday**: Warm up followed by workout #25
- **Tuesday**: Warm up followed by workout #26
- **Wednesday**: Rest
- **Thursday**: Warm up followed by workout #28
- **Friday**: Warm up followed by workout #28
- **Saturday**: Rest
- **Sunday**: Rest

CHAPTER 7

Cardio for Seniors

"It does not matter how slowly you go as long as you do not stop."

Confucius

Balance is essential, but you can't perform balance exercises every day. You need to rest your muscles. But what do you do on your days off if you still want to train? Cardio is a great option and has many benefits for seniors.

In this chapter, we will take a look at some of the benefits of cardio for seniors, and we will take a look at what cardio exercises are your best options.

What are the Benefits of Cardio for Seniors?

Incorporating cardio into your life has hundreds of benefits, but most are not cardio-specific. Here are five specific benefits to adding cardio workouts into your week.

Benefit #1 Reduced Risk of Heart Disease

One of the leading causes of death among seniors is heart disease, particularly in men. However, studies have shown that frequent cardiovascular exercise can help to reduce the risk of heart disease-related mortality in seniors [15].

If your doctor has told you to take care of your heart, adding cardio to your lifestyle could do wonders.

Benefit #2 Increased Cognition

The relationship between cardiovascular exercise and cognition in seniors is well established; the exact reason is unknown, though many theories exist. Increased blood flow to the brain, reduced inflammation, increased socialisation (running clubs, exercise classes etc.), and improved mental health are all benefits of cardiovascular exercise that could explain why cognition improves.

Benefit #3 Reduces Fall Risk

The idea that running or cycling could reduce your risk of falling may feel counterintuitive. Images of slipping in the mud or tripping over a root are probably going through your head. But provided you are performing your cardio in safe spaces, the movement can help with coordination, mobility, and agility, making you less likely to fall over in your daily life.

Benefit #4 Increased Strength

If you embark on your new training regime, you are unlikely to have powerful muscles. However, there is evidence that cardiovascular exercise can increase muscle size and strength in untrained individuals. You will build strength by following the balance workouts, but adding cardio can also help, particularly with leg muscles.

Benefit #5 Weight Loss

Any exercise will burn calories, and long cardio sessions are excellent. If you want to lose some body fat, then

2-3 extra cardio sessions could help as they could help burn over 600 calories for the week.

Types of Cardiovascular Exercise

There are many different forms of cardio available, but here is a quick list of several forms of cardio ideal for seniors looking to improve their fitness and balance. Of course, if you have limited mobility, your options will be fewer, but if you have medium or high mobility, then all of the options below should be fine.

Walking/Hiking

This is the most accessible form of cardio available, and it is a perfect way to burn calories and improve your fitness even if you have limited mobility. Try walking briskly, as this is the most effective form of walking. Hiking is a little different, the terrain is more challenging (though often very beautiful), and some readers may struggle. But hiking is fantastic for your mood and is great to do with friends and family.

Sports

Sure, many sports may not be suitable for many seniors, boxing, for example! But an abundance of sports has been created with seniors in mind, all of which can burn calories and improve your fitness.

- Tennis, badminton, pickleball
- Walking versions of popular sports: walking football, walking basketball
- Bowls, ten-pin bowling, boules

The competitive and cooperative side of these sports can really help you to perform at a higher intensity than you might otherwise. Also, the social side can be very beneficial.

Swimming/Water Aerobics

Swimming and pool-related exercise classes are a great option for seniors as they are very low-impact, making it perfect if you have mobility issues. That doesn't mean that you can attempt the butterfly, but simple swimming strokes such as breaststroke or backstroke are pretty safe to perform and great for your fitness.

Cardio Machines

If you feel that exercising outdoors is a little risky, then using cardio machines is a great option. You can either purchase your own for home use or use the machines at the gym.

- Treadmill
- Exercise bike
- Elliptical trainer
- Recumbent bike
- Rower

Cardio machines are very safe, they can also be paired with heart rate monitors so that you stay in the ideal training zone, and some machines, such as the recumbent bike, are perfect for people with mobility issues.

Jogging

The simple act of putting some running shoes on and going for a jog around your local neighbourhood can be a game changer for many people. Provided that they have the mobility to do so. Jogging is free (other than shoe costs), requires no fancy equipment, and can be taken up very easily. Just tie your laces and walk out of your front door.

Cycling

Though not quite as accessible or cost-effective as jogging, cycling can be a lot of fun, and it allows you to travel at much faster speeds. Just make sure that you are staying safe and that you know the local laws regarding cycling in your area.

How Often Should You Perform Cardio?

Depending on the intensity, you can perform cardio anywhere from once to seven times per week. Walking should be performed every day if possible. At the same time, higher-intensity exercises such as cycling or jogging should depend on how you feel on the day, how often you have trained recently, and how well your recovery is going.

Your mobility level will also influence how often you perform cardio. For example, even walking may feel like an intense workout for someone with minimal mobility. In this case, you may need rest periods in between.

A good rule for most readers would be to avoid higher-intensity cardio when you perform resistance workouts. But a 30-60 minute walk on training days is acceptable any day.

CHAPTER 8

Eight Week Home Workout for Seniors with Limited Mobility

This workout is designed for people training at home who have limited mobility. The workout will require that you own a sturdy chair and a resistance band, and it will provide both chair and body weight exercises. If you find any exercise too strenuous simply omit it from the workout. Cardio will involve walking outside, but if you own a cardio machine (treadmill, elliptical, bike, rower) and you feel capable of using it safely, then, by all means, use that.

For the first two weeks, you will only train twice weekly, with cardio as an optional workout on the non-training days. The first few weeks of training often cause muscle pain (DOMS), and extra recovery time will be needed if you feel fine. Repeat one (or both) of the sessions to bring your weekly total to four.

This program is designed to get progressively more challenging as the weeks go by. As this is a bodyweight (and chair) workout, that means increasing the number of reps performed. But if you are struggling to reach the lower end of the rep range, go back a couple of weeks and repeat.

Warm-Up

The following warm-up should be performed at the start of every workout. But to keep the workout table simple, it will be referred to as "Warm-Up Program" for each session.

Exercise	Sets	Reps	Rest Between Sets
Neck Warm Up	1	6	n/a
Shoulder Shrugs	1	5	n/a
Shoulder Rolls	1	5	n/a
Arm Circles	1	10	n/a
High Knees	1 (each leg)	5-10	30 seconds
Reverse Knees	1 (each leg)	5-10	30 seconds
Calf Raises	1	10	n/a

Exercises

- Box Squat (exercise #1)
- Seated Leg Extension (exercise #6)
- Seated Leg Extension with ankle weights (exercise #7)
- Seated Hamstring Curls (exercise #13)
- Seated Hamstring Curls with Resistance Band (exercise #14)
- Standing Hip Extension (exercise #15)
- Standing Hip Extension with Ankle Weights (exercise #16)
- Single Leg Stand – Knee Forward (exercise #17)
- Single Leg Stand – Heel Back (exercise #18)
- Lateral Lunges (exercise #22)
- Sit and Reach (exercise #26)
- Seated Resistance Band Bicep Curl (exercise #29)
- Seated Toe Taps (exercise #30)
- Wall Push-Ups (exercise #31)
- Box Push-Ups (exercise #32)
- Rock the Boat (exercise #37)
- Marching in Place (exercise #38)
- Side Lying Leg Circles (exercise #42)

While all the exercises included in each workout routine below can be accessed individually by scanning their respective QR codes, **if you wish to see all the exercises included in a workout in a single video**, avoiding the necessity of scanning each exercise's QR code one at a time, become part of our community by scanning this QR code.

SCAN FOR VIDEO

Seniors with Limited Mobility – Workouts Week One

(2 *workouts*)

Week One – Workout #1

Exercise	Sets	Reps	Rest	Exercise Number
Warm Up Session				
Seated Hamstring Curls	3 (each leg)	10	30 seconds	#14
Box Squat	3	10	30 seconds	#1
Lateral Lunges	2 (each leg)	10	30 seconds	#22
Wall Push-Ups	3	10	30 seconds	#31
Rock the Boat	2 (each leg)	30 secs	30 seconds	#37
Sit and Reach	2 (each leg)	10	30 seconds	#26

Week One – Workout #2

Exercise	Sets	Reps	Rest	Exercise Number
Warm Up Session				
Seated Hamstring Curls with Resistance Band	3 (each leg)	10	30 seconds	#14
Box Squat	3	10	30 seconds	#1
Seated Leg Extension	3 (each leg)	10	30 seconds	#6

Exercise	**Sets**	**Reps**	**Rest**	**Exercise Number**
Warm Up Session				
Standing Hip Extension	2 (each leg)	10	30 seconds	#15
Box Push-Ups	3	10	30 seconds	#32
Seated Toe Taps	3	10	30 seconds	#30

Seniors with Limited Mobility – Workouts Week Two

(2 *workouts*)

Week Two - Workout #1

Exercise	**Sets**	**Reps**	**Rest**	**Exercise Number**
		Warm Up Session		
Seated Hamstring Curls	3 (each leg)	10	30 seconds	#14
Box Squat	3	10	30 seconds	#1
Lateral Lunges	2 (each leg)	10	30 seconds	#22
Wall Push-Ups	3	10	30 seconds	#31
Rock the Boat	2 (each leg)	30 secs	30 seconds	#37
Sit and Reach	2 (each leg)	10	30 seconds	#26

Week Two - Workout #2

Exercise	**Sets**	**Reps**	**Rest**	**Exercise Number**
		Warm Up Session		
Seated Hamstring Curls with Resistance Band	3 (each leg)	10	30 seconds	#14
Box Squat	3	10	30 seconds	#1
Seated Leg Extension	3 (each leg)	10	30 seconds	#6

Exercise	**Sets**	**Reps**	**Rest**	**Exercise Number**
Warm Up Session				
Standing Hip Extension	2 (each leg)	10	30 seconds	#15
Box Push-Ups	3	10	30 seconds	#32
Seated Toe Taps	3	10	30 seconds	#30

Seniors with Limited Mobility – Workouts Week Three

(*4 workouts*)

Week Three – Workout #1

Exercise	Sets	Reps	Rest	Exercise Number
Warm Up Session				
Seated Hamstring Curls	3 (each leg)	10	30 seconds	#14
Box Squat	3	10	30 seconds	#1
Lateral Lunges	2 (each leg)	10	30 seconds	#22
Wall Push-Ups	3	10	30 seconds	#31
Rock the Boat	2 (each leg)	30 secs	30 seconds	#37
Sit and Reach	2 (each leg)	10	30 seconds	#26

Week Three – Workout #2

Exercise	Sets	Reps	Rest	Exercise Number
Warm Up Session				
Single Leg Stand Knee Forward	2 (each leg)	10	30 seconds	#17
Single Leg Stand Heel Back	2 (each leg)	10	30 seconds	#18
Seated Calf Raises	3	10	30 seconds	#11

Exercise	Sets	Reps	Rest	Exercise Number
Warm Up Session				
Standing Hip Extension	2 (each leg)	10	30 seconds	#15
Box Push-Ups	3	10	30 seconds	#32
Seated Resistance Band Bicep Curl	3	10	30 seconds	#29

Week Three – Workout #3

Exercise	Sets	Reps	Rest	Exercise Number
Warm Up Session				
Seated Hamstring Curls with Resistance Band	3 (each leg)	10	30 seconds	#14
Box Squat	3	10	30 seconds	#1
Seated Leg Extension	3 (each leg)	10	30 seconds	#6
Standing Hip Extension	2 (each leg)	10	30 seconds	#15
Box Push-Ups	3	10	30 seconds	#32
Seated Toe Taps	3	10	30 seconds	#30

Week Three – Workout #4

Exercise	Sets	Reps	Rest	Exercise Number
Warm Up Session				
Seated Leg Extension with Ankle Weight	3 (each leg)	10	30 seconds	#7
Box Squat	3	10	30 seconds	#1
Marching in Place	3	30 secs	30 seconds	#38
Side Lying Leg Circles	2 (each leg)	10	30-60 seconds	#42
Wall Push-Ups	3	10	30 seconds	#31
Sit and Reach	2 (each leg)	10	30 seconds	#26

Seniors with Limited Mobility – Workouts Week Four

(*4 workouts*)

Week Four – Workout #1

Exercise	Sets	Reps	Rest	Exercise Number
Warm Up Session				
Seated Hamstring Curls	3 (each leg)	10	30 seconds	#14
Box Squat	3	10	30 seconds	#1
Lateral Lunges	2 (each leg)	10	30 seconds	#22
Wall Push-Ups	3	10	30 seconds	#31
Rock the Boat	2 (each leg)	30 secs	30 seconds	#37
Sit and Reach	2 (each leg)	10	30 seconds	#26

Week Four – Workout #2

Exercise	Sets	Reps	Rest	Exercise Number
Warm Up Session				
Single Leg Stand Knee Forward	2 (each leg)	10	30 seconds	#17
Single Leg Stand Heel Back	2 (each leg)	10	30 seconds	#18
Seated Calf Raises	3	10	30 seconds	#11

Exercise	Sets	Reps	Rest	Exercise Number
Warm Up Session				
Standing Hip Extension	2 (each leg)	10	30 seconds	#15
Box Push-Ups	3	10	30 seconds	#32
Seated Resistance Band Bicep Curl	3	10	30 seconds	#29

Week Four – Workout #3

Exercise	Sets	Reps	Rest	Exercise Number
Warm Up Session				
Seated Hamstring Curls with Resistance Band	3 (each leg)	10	30 seconds	#14
Box Squat	3	10	30 seconds	#1
Seated Leg Extension	3 (each leg)	10	30 seconds	#6
Standing Hip Extension	2 (each leg)	10	30 seconds	#15
Box Push-Ups	3	10	30 seconds	#32
Seated Toe Taps	3	10	30 seconds	#30

Week Four – Workout #4

Exercise	Sets	Reps	Rest	Exercise Number
Warm Up Session				
Seated Leg Extension with Ankle Weight	3 (each leg)	10	30 seconds	#7
Box Squat	3	10	30 seconds	#1
Marching in Place	3	30 secs	30 seconds	#38
Side Lying Leg Circles	2 (each leg)	10	30-60 seconds	#42
Wall Push-Ups	3	10	30 seconds	#31
Sit and Reach	2 (each leg)	10	30 seconds	#26

Seniors with Limited Mobility – Workouts Week Five

(*4 workouts*)

Week Five – Workout #1

Exercise	**Sets**	**Reps**	**Rest**	**Exercise Number**
		Warm Up Session		
Seated Hamstring Curls	3 (each leg)	10-15	30 seconds	#14
Box Squat	3	10-15	30 seconds	#1
Lateral Lunges	2 (each leg)	10-12	30 seconds	#22
Wall Push-Ups	3	10-15	30 seconds	#31
Rock the Boat	2 (each leg)	30 secs	30 seconds	#37
Sit and Reach	2 (each leg)	10-12	30 seconds	#26

Week Five – Workout #2

Exercise	**Sets**	**Reps**	**Rest**	**Exercise Number**
		Warm Up Session		
Single Leg Stand Knee Forward	2 (each leg)	10-15	30 seconds	#17
Single Leg Stand Heel Back	2 (each leg)	10-15	30 seconds	#18
Seated Calf Raises	3	10-15	30 seconds	#11

Exercise	Sets	Reps	Rest	Exercise Number
Warm Up Session				
Standing Hip Extension	2 (each leg)	10-12	30 seconds	#15
Box Push-Ups	3	10-15	30 seconds	#32
Seated Resistance Band Bicep Curl	3	10-12	30 seconds	#29

Week Five – Workout #3

Exercise	Sets	Reps	Rest	Exercise Number
Warm Up Session				
Seated Hamstring Curls with Resistance Band	3 (each leg)	10-15	30 seconds	#14
Box Squat	3	10-15	30 seconds	#1
Seated Leg Extension	3 (each leg)	10-12	30 seconds	#6
Standing Hip Extension	2 (each leg)	10-12	30 seconds	#15
Box Push-Ups	3	10-15	30 seconds	#32
Seated Toe Taps	3	10-15	30 seconds	#30

Week Five – Workout #4

Exercise	Sets	Reps	Rest	Exercise Number
Warm Up Session				
Seated Leg Extension with Ankle Weight	3 (each leg)	10-15	30 seconds	#7
Box Squat	3	10-15	30 seconds	#1
Marching in Place	3	40 secs	30 seconds	#38
Side Lying Leg Circles	2 (each leg)	10-15	30-60 seconds	#42
Wall Push-Ups	3	10-15	30 seconds	#31
Sit and Reach	2 (each leg)	10-15	30 seconds	#26

Seniors with Limited Mobility – Workouts Week Six

(*4 workouts*)

Week Six – Workout #1

Exercise	Sets	Reps	Rest	Exercise Number
Warm Up Session				
Seated Hamstring Curls	3 (each leg)	12-20	30 seconds	#14
Box Squat	3	12-20	30 seconds	#1
Lateral Lunges	2 (each leg)	12	30 seconds	#22
Wall Push-Ups	3	12-20	30 seconds	#31
Rock the Boat	2 (each leg)	40 secs	30 seconds	#37
Sit and Reach	2 (each leg)	12-20	30 seconds	#26

Week Six – Workout #2

Exercise	Sets	Reps	Rest	Exercise Number
Warm Up Session				
Single Leg Stand Knee Forward	2 (each leg)	12	30 seconds	#17
Single Leg Stand Heel Back	2 (each leg)	12	30 seconds	#18
Seated Calf Raises	3	12-20	30 seconds	#11

Exercise	**Sets**	**Reps**	**Rest**	**Exercise Number**
Warm Up Session				
Standing Hip Extension	2 (each leg)	12	30 seconds	#15
Box Push-Ups	3	12-20	30 seconds	#32
Seated Resistance Band Bicep Curl	3	12-20	30 seconds	#29

Week Six – Workout #3

Exercise	**Sets**	**Reps**	**Rest**	**Exercise Number**
Warm Up Session				
Seated Hamstring Curls with Resistance Band	3 (each leg)	12-20	30 seconds	#14
Box Squat	3	12-20	30 seconds	#1
Seated Leg Extension	3 (each leg)	12	30 seconds	#6
Standing Hip Extension	2 (each leg)	12	30 seconds	#15
Box Push-Ups	3	12-20	30 seconds	#32
Seated Toe Taps	3	12-20	30 seconds	#30

Week Six – Workout #4

Exercise	Sets	Reps	Rest	Exercise Number
Warm Up Session				
Seated Leg Extension with Ankle Weight	3 (each leg)	12-20	30 seconds	#7
Box Squat	3	12-20	30 seconds	#1
Marching in Place	3	60 secs	30 seconds	#38
Side Lying Leg Circles	2 (each leg)	12-20	30-60 seconds	#42
Wall Push-Ups	3	12-20	30 seconds	#31
Sit and Reach	2 (each leg)	12-20	30 seconds	#26

Seniors with Limited Mobility – Workouts Week Seven

(*4 workouts*)

Week Seven – Workout #1

Exercise	Sets	Reps	Rest	Exercise Number
Warm Up Session				
Seated Hamstring Curls	3 (each leg)	15	30 seconds	#14
Box Squat	3	15-20	30 seconds	#1
Lateral Lunges	2 (each leg)	15	30 seconds	#22
Wall Push-Ups	3	15-20	30 seconds	#31
Rock the Boat	2 (each leg)	60 secs	30 seconds	#37
Sit and Reach	2 (each leg)	15	30 seconds	#26

Week Seven – Workout #2

Exercise	Sets	Reps	Rest	Exercise Number
Warm Up Session				
Single Leg Stand Knee Forward	2 (each leg)	15	30 seconds	#17
Single Leg Stand Heel Back	2 (each leg)	15	30 seconds	#18
Seated Calf Raises	3	15-20	30 seconds	#11

Exercise	Sets	Reps	Rest	Exercise Number
Warm Up Session				
Standing Hip Extension	2 (each leg)	15	30 seconds	#15
Box Push-Ups	3	15-20	30 seconds	#32
Seated Resistance Band Bicep Curl	3	15-20	30 seconds	#29

Week Seven – Workout #3

Exercise	Sets	Reps	Rest	Exercise Number
Warm Up Session				
Seated Hamstring Curls with Resistance Band	3 (each leg)	15-20	30 seconds	#14
Box Squat	3	15-20	30 seconds	#1
Seated Leg Extension	3 (each leg)	15	30 seconds	#6
Standing Hip Extension	2 (each leg)	15	30 seconds	#15
Box Push-Ups	3	15-20	30 seconds	#32
Seated Toe Taps	3	15-20	30 seconds	#30

Week Seven – Workout #4

Exercise	**Sets**	**Reps**	**Rest**	**Exercise Number**
Warm Up Session				
Seated Leg Extension with Ankle Weight	3 (each leg)	15	30 seconds	#7
Box Squat	3	15-20	30 seconds	#1
Marching in Place	3	75 secs	30 seconds	#38
Side Lying Leg Circles	2 (each leg)	15	30-60 seconds	#42
Wall Push-Ups	3	15-20	30 seconds	#31
Sit and Reach	2 (each leg)	15	30 seconds	#26

Seniors with Limited Mobility – Workouts Week Eight

(*4 workouts*)

Week Eight – Workout #1

Exercise	Sets	Reps	Rest	Exercise Number
Warm Up Session				
Seated Hamstring Curls	3 (each leg)	15	30 seconds	#14
Box Squat	3	20	30 seconds	#1
Lateral Lunges	2 (each leg)	15	30 seconds	#22
Wall Push-Ups	3	20	30 seconds	#31
Rock the Boat	2 (each leg)	75 secs	30 seconds	#37
Sit and Reach	2 (each leg)	20	30 seconds	#26

Week Eight – Workout #2

Exercise	Sets	Reps	Rest	Exercise Number
Warm Up Session				
Single Leg Stand Knee Forward	2 (each leg)	15	30 seconds	#17
Single Leg Stand Heel Back	2 (each leg)	15	30 seconds	#18
Seated Calf Raises	3	20	30 seconds	#11

Exercise	Sets	Reps	Rest	Exercise Number
Warm Up Session				
Standing Hip Extension	2 (each leg)	15	30 seconds	#15
Box Push-Ups	3	20	30 seconds	#32
Seated Resistance Band Bicep Curl	3	20	30 seconds	#29

Week Eight – Workout #3

Exercise	Sets	Reps	Rest	Exercise Number
Warm Up Session				
Seated Hamstring Curls with Resistance Band	3 (each leg)	20	30 seconds	#14
Box Squat	3	20	30 seconds	#1
Seated Leg Extension	3 (each leg)	15	30 seconds	#6
Standing Hip Extension	2 (each leg)	15	30 seconds	#15
Box Push-Ups	3	20	30 seconds	#32
Seated Toe Taps	3	20	30 seconds	#30

Week Eight – Workout #4

Exercise	Sets	Reps	Rest	Exercise Number
Warm Up Session				
Seated Leg Extension with Ankle Weight	3 (each leg)	15	30 seconds	#7
Box Squat	3	20	30 seconds	#1
Marching in Place	3	90 secs	30 seconds	#38
Side Lying Leg Circles	2 (each leg)	15	30-60 seconds	#42
Wall Push-Ups	3	20	30 seconds	#31
Sit and Reach	2 (each leg)	15	30 seconds	#26

Once you have completed this workout, it is a good idea to reassess your mobility score as well as your fitness. If your mobility has not improved, then repeat this eight week program, but aim for slightly higher reps.

If your mobility score *has* improved and you are feeling fitter and stronger, then you can progress to the medium mobility workout in the next chapter but there is no necessity to do so, if you feel comfortable with this workout routine then stick with it.

CHAPTER 9

Eight Week Home Workout for Seniors with Medium Mobility

This workout program is designed for seniors with medium mobility and decent fitness and strength levels. You will need a chair, resistance band, and ankle weights for this workout.

As with the previous workout, you will start with a couple of weeks of training twice per week (with optional cardio). This program is designed to get progressively more challenging each week. This will be done by increasing the number of reps that you perform. Just ensure that your form is still good.

If you can't hit the minimum number of reps for several exercises, then go back a couple of weeks and repeat them until you are strong enough.

Warm-Up

The following warm-up should be performed at the start of every workout. But to keep the workout table simple, it will be referred to as "Warm-Up Program" for each session.

Exercise	**Sets**	**Reps**	**Rest Between Sets**
Arm Circles	1 (each direction)	6	30 seconds
High Knees	1 (each leg)	5-10	30 seconds
Reverse Knees	1 (each leg)	5-10	30 seconds
Stair Climbing	1	30-60 seconds	n/a

Exercises

- Box Squat with Hands Raised Above Head (exercise #2)
- Seated Hamstring Curls (exercise #13)
- Seated Hamstring Curls with Resistance Band #14
- Single Leg Stand – Knee Forward (exercise #17)
- Single Leg Stand – Heel Back (exercise #18)

- Leg Swings - Forward & Back (exercise #19)
- Leg Swings – Side to Side (exercise #20)
- Lateral Lunges (exercise #22)
- Sumo Box Squat (exercise #29)
- Box Push-Ups (exercise #32)
- Knee Push-Ups (exercise #33)
- Bodyweight Squats (exercise #35)
- Bodyweight Sumo Squats (exercise #36)
- Marching in Place (exercise #38)
- Glute Bridges (exercise #39)
- Tricep Dips (exercise #43)
- Plank (exercise #44)
- Reverse Abdominal Crunches (exercise #46)
- Wood Chops (exercise #47)
- Superman (exercise #48)
- Dead Bugs (exercise #49)
- Bird Dog (exercise #50)

While all the exercises included in each workout routine below can be accessed individually by scanning their respective QR codes, **if you wish to see all the exercises included in a workout in a single video**, avoiding the necessity of scanning each exercise's QR code one at a time, become part of our community by scanning this QR code.

SCAN FOR VIDEO

Seniors with Medium Mobility – Workouts Week One

(2 *workouts*)

Week One – Workout #1

Exercise	Sets	Reps	Rest	Exercise Number
Warm Up Session				
Seated Hamstring Curls with Resistance Band	3 (each leg)	8-10	30 seconds	#14
Box Squats with Hands Raised	3	10	30 seconds	#2
Lateral Lunges	2 (each leg)	10	30 seconds	#22
Glute Bridges	3	10	30 seconds	#39
Knee Push-Ups	3	10	30-45 seconds	#33
Tricep Dips	3	10	30 seconds	#43
Reverse Abdominal Crunches	3	6-10	45 seconds	#46

Week One – Workout #2

Exercise	Sets	Reps	Rest	Exercise Number
Warm Up Session				
Leg Swings – Forward Back	2 (each leg)	10	30-60 seconds	#19
Leg Swings – Side to Side	2 (each leg)	10	30-60 seconds	#20
Sumo Box Squat	3	10	30 seconds	#29
Marching in Place	3	60 secs	30 seconds	#38
Knee Push-Ups	3	10	30-45 seconds	#33
Wood Chops	2 (each arm)	10	45 seconds	#47
Plank	3	30 secs	45-60 seconds	#44

Seniors with Medium Mobility – Workouts Week Two

(2 *workouts*)

Week Two – Workout #1

Exercise	Sets	Reps	Rest	Exercise Number
Warm Up Session				
Seated Hamstring Curls	3 (each leg)	10	30 seconds	#13
Bodyweight Sumo Squats	3	10	30 seconds	#36
Glute Bridges	3	10	30 seconds	#39
Lateral Lunges	3 (each leg)	10	30 seconds	#22
Knee Push Ups	3	10	30-45 seconds	#33
Tricep Dips	3	10	30 seconds	#43
Bird Dog	3	10	30 seconds	#50

Week Two – Workout #2

Exercise	Sets	Reps	Rest	Exercise Number
Warm Up Session				
Single Leg Stand Knee Forward	2 (each leg)	10	30 seconds	#17
Single Leg Stand Heel Back	2 (each leg)	10	30 seconds	#18

Exercise	Sets	Reps	Rest	Exercise Number
Warm Up Session				
Bodyweight Squat	3	10	30 seconds	#35
Box Push-Ups	3	10	30 seconds	#32
Knee Push-Ups	3	10	30-45 seconds	#33
Dead Bugs	3	10	30 seconds	#49
Superman	3	10	30 seconds	#48

Seniors with Medium Mobility – Workouts Week Three

(4 *workouts*)

Week Three – Workout #1

Exercise	Sets	Reps	Rest	Exercise Number
Warm Up Session				
Seated Hamstring Curls with Resistance Band	3 (each leg)	8-10	30 seconds	#14
Box Squats with Hands Raised	3	10	30 seconds	#2
Lateral Lunges	2 (each leg)	10	30 seconds	#22
Glute Bridges	3	10	30 seconds	#39
Knee Push-Ups	3	10	30-45 seconds	#33
Tricep Dips	3	10	30 seconds	#43
Reverse Abdominal Crunches	3	6-10	45 seconds	#46

Week Three – Workout #2

Exercise	Sets	Reps	Rest	Exercise Number
Warm Up Session				
Leg Swings – Forward Back	2 (each leg)	10	30-60 seconds	#19
Leg Swings – Side to Side	2 (each leg)	10	30-60 seconds	#20
Sumo Box Squat	3	10	30 seconds	#29
Marching in Place	3	60 secs	30 seconds	#38
Knee Push-Ups	3	10	30-45 seconds	#33
Wood Chops	2 (each arm)	10	45 seconds	#47
Plank	3	30 secs	45-60 seconds	#44

Week Three – Workout #3

Exercise	Sets	Reps	Rest	Exercise Number
Warm Up Session				
Seated Hamstring Curls	3 (each leg)	10	30 seconds	#13
Bodyweight Sumo Squats	3	10	30 seconds	#36
Glute Bridges	3	10	30 seconds	#39
Lateral Lunges	3 (each leg)	10	30 seconds	#22
Knee Push-Ups	3	10	30-45 seconds	#33
Tricep Dips	3	10	30 seconds	#43
Bird Dog	3	10	30 seconds	#50

Week Three – Workout #4

Exercise	Sets	Reps	Rest	Exercise Number
Warm Up Session				
Single Leg Stand Knee Forward	2 (each leg)	10	30 seconds	#17
Single Leg Stand Heel Back	2 (each leg)	10	30 seconds	#18
Bodyweight Squat	3	10	30 seconds	#35
Box Push-Ups	3	10	30 seconds	#32
Knee Push-Ups	3	10	30-45 seconds	#33
Dead Bugs	3	10	30 seconds	#49
Superman	3	10	30 seconds	#48

Seniors with Medium Mobility – Workouts Week Four

(4 *workouts*)

Week Four – Workout #1

Exercise	Sets	Reps	Rest	Exercise Number
Warm Up Session				
Seated Hamstring Curls with Resistance Band	3 (each leg)	12	30 seconds	#14
Box Squats with Hands Raised	3	10-15	30 seconds	#2
Lateral Lunges	2 (each leg)	10-15	30 seconds	#22
Glute Bridges	3	10-15	30 seconds	#39
Knee Push-Ups	3	10-15	30-45 seconds	#33
Tricep Dips	3	10-15	30 seconds	#43
Reverse Abdominal Crunches	3	10	45 seconds	#46

Week Four – Workout #2

Exercise	Sets	Reps	Rest	Exercise Number
Warm Up Session				
Leg Swings – Forward Back	2 (each leg)	12	30-60 seconds	#19
Leg Swings – Side to Side	2 (each leg)	12	30-60 seconds	#20
Sumo Box Squat	3	10-15	30 seconds	#29
Marching in Place	3	75 secs	30 seconds	#38
Knee Push-Ups	3	10-15	30-45 seconds	#33
Wood Chops	2 (each arm)	10-15	45 seconds	#47
Plank	3	30 secs	45 seconds	#44

Week Four – Workout #3

Exercise	Sets	Reps	Rest	Exercise Number
Warm Up Session				
Seated Hamstring Curls	3 (each leg)	12	30 seconds	#13
Bodyweight Sumo Squats	3	10-15	30 seconds	#36
Glute Bridges	3	10-15	30 seconds	#39
Lateral Lunges	3 (each leg)	12	30 seconds	#22
Knee Push-Ups	3	10-15	30-45 seconds	#33
Tricep Dips	3	10-15	30 seconds	#43
Bird Dog	3	10-15	30 seconds	#50

Week Four – Workout #4

Exercise	Sets	Reps	Rest	Exercise Number
Warm Up Session				
Single Leg Stand Knee Forward	2 (each leg)	12	30 seconds	#17
Single Leg Stand Heel Back	2 (each leg)	12	30 seconds	#18
Bodyweight Squat	3	10-15	30 seconds	#35
Box Push-Ups	3	10-15	30 seconds	#32
Knee Push-Ups	3	10-15	30-45 seconds	#33
Dead Bugs	3	10-15	30 seconds	#49
Superman	3	10-15	30 seconds	#48

Seniors with Medium Mobility – Workouts Week Five

(4 *workouts*)

Week Five – Workout #1

Exercise	Sets	Reps	Rest	Exercise Number
Warm Up Session				
Seated Hamstring Curls with Resistance Band	3 (each leg)	15	30 seconds	#14
Box Squats with Hands Raised	3	15	30 seconds	#2
Lateral Lunges	2 (each leg)	15	30 seconds	#22
Glute Bridges	3	15	30 seconds	#39
Knee Push-Ups	3	15	30-45 seconds	#33
Tricep Dips	3	15	30 seconds	#43
Reverse Abdominal Crunches	3	15	45 seconds	#46

Week Five – Workout #2

Exercise	Sets	Reps	Rest	Exercise Number
Warm Up Session				
Leg Swings – Forward Back	2 (each leg)	15	30-60 seconds	#19
Leg Swings – Side to Side	2 (each leg)	15	30-60 seconds	#20
Sumo Box Squat	3	15	30 seconds	#29
Marching in Place	3	90 secs	30 seconds	#38
Knee Push-Ups	3	15	30-45 seconds	#33
Wood Chops	2 (each arm)	15	45 seconds	#47
Plank	4	30 secs	45 seconds	#44

Week Five – Workout #3

Exercise	Sets	Reps	Rest	Exercise Number
Warm Up Session				
Seated Hamstring Curls	3 (each leg)	15	30 seconds	#13
Bodyweight Sumo Squats	3	15	30 seconds	#36
Glute Bridges	3	15	30 seconds	#39
Lateral Lunges	3 (each leg)	15	30 seconds	#22
Knee Push-Ups	3	15	30-45 seconds	#33
Tricep Dips	3	15	30 seconds	#43
Bird Dog	3	15	30 seconds	#50

Week Five – Workout #4

Exercise	Sets	Reps	Rest	Exercise Number
Warm Up Session				
Single Leg Stand Knee Forward	2 (each leg)	15	30 seconds	#17
Single Leg Stand Heel Back	2 (each leg)	15	30 seconds	#18
Bodyweight Squat	3	15	30 seconds	#35
Box Push-Ups	3	15	30 seconds	#32
Knee Push-Ups	3	15	30-45 seconds	#33
Dead Bugs	3	15	30 seconds	#49
Superman	3	15	30 seconds	#48

Seniors with Medium Mobility – Workouts Week Six

(4 *workouts*)

Week Six – Workout #1

Exercise	**Sets**	**Reps**	**Rest**	**Exercise Number**
Warm Up Session				
Seated Hamstring Curls with Resistance Band	3 (each leg)	15	30 seconds	#14
Box Squats with Hands Raised	3	15-20	30 seconds	#2
Lateral Lunges	2 (each leg)	15	30 seconds	#22
Glute Bridges	3	15-20	30 seconds	#39
Knee Push-Ups	3	15-20	30-45 seconds	#33
Tricep Dips	3	15-20	30 seconds	#43
Reverse Abdominal Crunches	3	15	45 seconds	#46

Week Six – Workout #2

Exercise	Sets	Reps	Rest	Exercise Number
Warm Up Session				
Leg Swings – Forward Back	2 (each leg)	15	30-60 seconds	#19
Leg Swings – Side to Side	2 (each leg)	15	30-60 seconds	#20
Sumo Box Squat	3	15-20	30 seconds	#29
Marching in Place	3	90 secs	30 seconds	#38
Knee Push-Ups	3	15-20	30-45 seconds	#33
Wood Chops	2 (each arm)	15	45 seconds	#47
Plank	4	30 secs	45 seconds	#44

Week Six – Workout #3

Exercise	Sets	Reps	Rest	Exercise Number
Warm Up Session				
Seated Hamstring Curls	3 (each leg)	15	30 seconds	#13
Bodyweight Sumo Squats	3	15-20	30 seconds	#36
Glute Bridges	3	15-20	30 seconds	#39
Lateral Lunges	3 (each leg)	15	30 seconds	#22
Knee Push-Ups	3	15-20	30-45 seconds	#33
Tricep Dips	3	15-20	30 seconds	#43
Bird Dog	3	15-20	30 seconds	#50

Week Six – Workout #4

Exercise	Sets	Reps	Rest	Exercise Number
Warm Up Session				
Single Leg Stand Knee Forward	2 (each leg)	15	30 seconds	#17
Single Leg Stand Heel Back	2 (each leg)	15	30 seconds	#18
Bodyweight Squat	3	15-20	30 seconds	#35
Box Push-Ups	3	15-20	30 seconds	#32
Knee Push-Ups	3	15-20	30-45 seconds	#33
Dead Bugs	3	15-20	30 seconds	#49
Superman	3	15-20	30 seconds	#48

Seniors with Medium Mobility – Workouts Week Seven

(4 *workouts*)

Week Seven – Workout #1

Exercise	Sets	Reps	Rest	Exercise Number
Warm Up Session				
Seated Hamstring Curls with Resistance Band	3 (each leg)	15	30 seconds	#14
Box Squats with Hands Raised	3	15-20	30 seconds	#2
Lateral Lunges	2 (each leg)	15	30 seconds	#22
Glute Bridges	3	15-20	30 seconds	#39
Knee Push-Ups	3	15-20	30-45 seconds	#33
Tricep Dips	3	15-20	30 seconds	#43
Reverse Abdominal Crunches	3	15	45 seconds	#46

Week Seven – Workout #2

Exercise	Sets	Reps	Rest	Exercise Number
Warm Up Session				
Leg Swings – Forward Back	2 (each leg)	15	30-60 seconds	#19
Leg Swings – Side to Side	2 (each leg)	15	30-60 seconds	#20
Sumo Box Squat	3	15-20	30 seconds	#29
Marching in Place	3	90 secs	30 seconds	#38
Knee Push-Ups	3	15-20	30-45 seconds	#33
Wood Chops	2 (each arm)	15	45 seconds	#47
Plank	5	30 secs	45 seconds	#44

Week Seven – Workout #3

Exercise	Sets	Reps	Rest	Exercise Number
Warm Up Session				
Seated Hamstring Curls	3 (each leg)	15	30 seconds	#13
Bodyweight Sumo Squats	3	15-20	30 seconds	#36
Glute Bridges	3	15-20	30 seconds	#39
Lateral Lunges	3 (each leg)	15	30 seconds	#22
Knee Push-Ups	3	15-20	30-45 seconds	#33
Tricep Dips	3	15-20	30 seconds	#43
Bird Dog	3	15-20	30 seconds	#50

Week Seven – Workout #4

Exercise	Sets	Reps	Rest	Exercise Number
Warm Up Session				
Single Leg Stand Knee Forward	2 (each leg)	15	30 seconds	#17
Single Leg Stand Heel Back	2 (each leg)	15	30 seconds	#18
Bodyweight Squat	3	15-20	30 seconds	#35
Box Push-Ups	3	15-20	30 seconds	#32
Knee Push-Ups	3	15-20	30-45 seconds	#33
Dead Bugs	3	15-20	30 seconds	#49
Superman	3	15-20	30 seconds	#48

Seniors with Medium Mobility – Workouts Week Eight

(4 *workouts*)

Week Eight – Workout #1

Exercise	Sets	Reps	Rest	Exercise Number
Warm Up Session				
Seated Hamstring Curls with Resistance Band	3 (each leg)	15	30 seconds	#14
Box Squats with Hands Raised	3	20	30 seconds	#2
Lateral Lunges	2 (each leg)	15	30 seconds	#22
Glute Bridges	3	20	30 seconds	#39
Knee Push-Ups	3	20	30-45 seconds	#33
Tricep Dips	3	20	30 seconds	#43
Reverse Abdominal Crunches	3	15	45 seconds	#46

Week Eight – Workout #2

Exercise	Sets	Reps	Rest	Exercise Number
Warm Up Session				
Leg Swings – Forward Back	2 (each leg)	15	30-60 seconds	#19
Leg Swings – Side to Side	2 (each leg)	15	30-60 seconds	#20
Sumo Box Squat	3	20	30 seconds	#29
Marching in Place	3	90 secs	30 seconds	#38
Knee Push-Ups	3	20	30-45 seconds	#33
Wood Chops	2 (each arm)	15	45 seconds	#47
Plank	5	30 secs	45 seconds	#44

Week Eight – Workout #3

Exercise	Sets	Reps	Rest	Exercise Number
Warm Up Session				
Seated Hamstring Curls	3 (each leg)	15	30 seconds	#13
Bodyweight Sumo Squats	3	20	30 seconds	#36
Glute Bridges	3	20	30 seconds	#39
Lateral Lunges	3 (each leg)	15	30 seconds	#22
Knee Push-Ups	3	20	30-45 seconds	#33
Tricep Dips	3	20	30 seconds	#43
Bird Dog	3	20	30 seconds	#50

Week Eight – Workout #4

Exercise	Sets	Reps	Rest	Exercise Number
Warm Up Session				
Single Leg Stand Knee Forward	2 (each leg)	15	30 seconds	#17
Single Leg Stand Heel Back	2 (each leg)	15	30 seconds	#18
Bodyweight Squat	3	20	30 seconds	#35
Box Push-Ups	3	20	30 seconds	#32
Knee Push-Ups	3	20	30-45 seconds	#33
Dead Bugs	3	20	30 seconds	#49
Superman	3	20	30 seconds	#48

CHAPTER 10

Eight Week Home Workout for Seniors with High Mobility

This workout is designed for seniors with a high degree of mobility and decent strength and fitness levels. You will need a sturdy chair, a resistance band, and some ankle weights for this workout.

If you find the workout too tricky, then drop down to the medium mobility workout in the previous chapter.

This workout will have four sessions per week, and they will be split into upper and lower-body workouts. Unlike the other eight-week workouts, this workout will not have two weeks of training twice per week.

Warm Up

This workout will use the high mobility warm-up from earlier, perform it at the beginning of each session. If you have a cardio machine then you can use that as well or instead.

Exercise	Sets	Reps	Rest Between Sets
Jogging on the Spot	1	30-60 seconds	n/a
Mountain Climbers	1	40-60 seconds	n/a
Lateral Lunges	1 (each leg)	10	30 seconds
Bodyweight Squats	2	10	30 seconds

Exercises

- Single Leg Box Squat (exercise #5)
- Seated Leg Extension with Ankle Weights (exercise #7)
- Seated Calf Raises (exercise #11)
- Seated Hamstring Curls (exercise #13)
- Seated Hamstring Curls with Resistance Band (exercise #14)
- Lateral Lunges (exercise #22)
- Squats while Holding Chair (exercise #23)

- Sumo Squats while Holding Chair (exercise #24)
- Single-Leg Romanian Deadlift (exercise #25)
- Seated Resistance Band Bicep Curl (exercise #29)
- Seated Toe Taps (exercise #30)
- Wall Push-Ups (exercise #31)
- Box Push-Ups (exercise #32)
- Knee Push-Ups (exercise #33)
- Push-Ups (exercise #34)
- Bodyweight Squats (exercise #35)
- Marching in Place (exercise #38)
- Glute Bridges (exercise #39)
- Lateral Lunges (exercise #40)
- Walking Lunges (exercise #41)
- Side Lying Leg Circles (exercise #42)
- Tricep Dips (exercise #43)
- Plank (exercise #44)
- Side Plank (exercise #45)
- Reverse Abdominal Crunches (exercise #46)
- Wood Chops (exercise #47)

While all the exercises included in each workout routine below can be accessed individually by scanning their respective QR codes, **if you wish to see all the exercises included in a workout in a single video**, avoiding the necessity of scanning each exercise's QR code one at a time, become part of our community by scanning this QR code.

SCAN FOR VIDEO

Seniors with High Mobility – Workouts Week One

(4 *workouts*)

Week One – Workout #1

Exercise	Sets	Reps	Rest	Exercise Number
Warm Up Session				
Seated Hamstring Curls with Resistance Band	3 (each leg)	10	30 seconds	#14
Sumo Squats while Holding Chair	3	10	60 seconds	#24
Seated Leg Extension with Ankle Weights	3 (each leg)	10	30 seconds	#7
Lateral Lunges	3 (each leg)	10	30 seconds	#40
Glute Bridges	3	10	30 seconds	#39
Seated Calf Raise	3	20	30 seconds	#11
Marching in Place	3	60 secs	30 seconds	#38

Week One – Workout #2

Exercise	Sets	Reps	Rest	Exercise Number
Warm Up Session				
Wall Push-Ups	3	10	30 seconds	#31
Push-Ups	3	1-10	60 seconds	#34
Knee Push-Ups	3	6-10	45 seconds	#33
Tricep Dips	3	6-10	30 seconds	#43
Side Lying Leg Circles	3 (each leg)	10	30 seconds	#42
Reverse Abdominal Crunches	3	6-10	45 seconds	#46
Side Plank	2 (each side)	30 secs	30 seconds	#45

Week One – Workout #3

Exercise	Sets	Reps	Rest	Exercise Number
Warm Up Session				
Seated Hamstring Curls	3 (each leg)	10	30 seconds	#13
Single Leg Box Squat	3 (each leg)	2	45 seconds	#5
Squats while Holding Chair	3	10	30 seconds	#23
Bodyweight Squats	3	10	30 seconds	#35

Exercise	Sets	Reps	Rest	Exercise Number
Warm Up Session				
Single-Leg Romanian Deadlifts	3 (each leg)	10	30 seconds	#25
Walking Lunges	4	10	60 seconds	#41
Lateral Lunges	3 (each leg)	10	30 seconds	#22

Week One – Workout #4

Exercise	Sets	Reps	Rest	Exercise Number
Warm Up Session				
Box Push-Ups	3	10	30 seconds	#32
Push-Ups	3	1-10	60 seconds	#34
Knee Push-Ups	3	6-10	45 seconds	#33
Seated Resistance Band Bicep Curl	3 (each arm)	10	30 seconds	#29
Seated Toe Taps	3	10	30-60 seconds	#30
Wood Chops	3 (each arm)	10	60-90 seconds	#47
Plank	3	30 secs	30 seconds	#44

Seniors with High Mobility – Workouts Week Two
(4 *workouts*)

Week Two – Workout #1

Exercise	Sets	Reps	Rest	Exercise Number
Warm Up Session				
Seated Hamstring Curls with Resistance Band	3 (each leg)	10	30 seconds	#14
Sumo Squats while Holding Chair	3	10	60 seconds	#24
Seated Leg Extension with Ankle Weights	3 (each leg)	10	30 seconds	#7
Lateral Lunges	3 (each leg)	10	30 seconds	#40
Glute Bridges	3	10	30 seconds	#39
Seated Calf Raise	3	20	30 seconds	#11
Marching in Place	3	60 secs	30 seconds	#38

Week Two – Workout #2

Exercise	Sets	Reps	Rest	Exercise Number
Warm Up Session				
Wall Push-Ups	3	10	30 seconds	#31
Push-Ups	3	1-10	60 seconds	#34
Knee Push-Ups	3	6-10	45 seconds	#33
Tricep Dips	3	6-10	30 seconds	#43
Side Lying Leg Circles	3 (each leg)	10	30 seconds	#42
Reverse Abdominal Crunches	3	6-10	45 seconds	#46
Side Plank	2 (each side)	30 secs	30 seconds	#45

Week Two – Workout #3

Exercise	Sets	Reps	Rest	Exercise Number
Warm Up Session				
Seated Hamstring Curls	3 (each leg)	10	30 seconds	#13
Single Leg Box Squat	3 (each leg)	3	45 seconds	#5
Squats while Holding Chair	3	10	30 seconds	#23
Bodyweight Squats	3	10	30 seconds	#35

Exercise	Sets	Reps	Rest	Exercise Number
Warm Up Session				
Single-Leg Romanian Deadlifts	3 (each leg)	10	30 seconds	#25
Walking Lunges	4	10	60 seconds	#41
Lateral Lunges	3 (each leg)	10	30 seconds	#22

Week Two – Workout #4

Exercise	Sets	Reps	Rest	Exercise Number
Warm Up Session				
Box Push-Ups	3	10	30 seconds	#32
Push-Ups	3	1-10	60 seconds	#34
Knee Push-Ups	3	6-10	45 seconds	#33
Seated Resistance Band Bicep Curl	3 (each arm)	10	30 seconds	#29
Seated Toe Taps	3	10	30-60 seconds	#30
Wood Chops	3 (each arm)	10	60-90 seconds	#47
Plank	3	30 secs	30 seconds	#44

Seniors with High Mobility – Workouts Week Three

(4 *workouts*)

Week Three – Workout #1

Exercise	Sets	Reps	Rest	Exercise Number
Warm Up Session				
Seated Hamstring Curls with Resistance Band	3 (each leg)	12	30 seconds	#14
Sumo Squats while Holding Chair	3	10-15	60 seconds	#24
Seated Leg Extension with Ankle Weights	3 (each leg)	12	30 seconds	#7
Lateral Lunges	3 (each leg)	12	30 seconds	#40
Glute Bridges	3	10-15	30 seconds	#39
Seated Calf Raise	3	20	30 seconds	#11
Marching in Place	3	90 secs	30 seconds	#38

Week Three – Workout #2

Exercise	Sets	Reps	Rest	Exercise Number
Warm Up Session				
Wall Push-Ups	3	10-15	30 seconds	#31
Push-Ups	3	1-12	60 seconds	#34
Knee Push-Ups	3	6-15	45 seconds	#33
Tricep Dips	3	6-15	30 seconds	#43
Side Lying Leg Circles	3 (each leg)	12	30 seconds	#42
Reverse Abdominal Crunches	3	6-12	45 seconds	#46
Side Plank	3 (each side)	30 secs	30 seconds	#45

Week Three – Workout #3

Exercise	Sets	Reps	Rest	Exercise Number
Warm Up Session				
Seated Hamstring Curls	3 (each leg)	12	30 seconds	#13
Single Leg Box Squat	3 (each leg)	3-5	45 seconds	#5
Squats while Holding Chair	3	10-15	30 seconds	#23
Bodyweight Squats	3	10-15	30 seconds	#35

Exercise	Sets	Reps	Rest	Exercise Number
Warm Up Session				
Single-Leg Romanian Deadlifts	3 (each leg)	12	30 seconds	#25
Walking Lunges	4	16	60 seconds	#41
Lateral Lunges	3 (each leg)	12	30 seconds	#22

Week Three – Workout #4

Exercise	Sets	Reps	Rest	Exercise Number
Warm Up Session				
Box Push-Ups	3	10-15	30 seconds	#32
Push-Ups	3	1-12	60 seconds	#34
Knee Push-Ups	3	6-12	45 seconds	#33
Seated Resistance Band Bicep Curl	3 (each arm)	12	30 seconds	#29
Seated Toe Taps	3	10-15	30-60 seconds	#30
Wood Chops	3 (each arm)	12	60-90 seconds	#47
Plank	3	30 secs	30 seconds	#44

Seniors with High Mobility – Workouts Week Four

(4 *workouts*)

Week Four – Workout #1

Exercise	Sets	Reps	Rest	Exercise Number
Warm Up Session				
Seated Hamstring Curls with Resistance Band	3 (each leg)	15	30 seconds	#14
Sumo Squats while Holding Chair	3	15-20	60 seconds	#24
Seated Leg Extension with Ankle Weights	3 (each leg)	15	30 seconds	#7
Lateral Lunges	3 (each leg)	15	30 seconds	#40
Glute Bridges	3	15-20	30 seconds	#39
Seated Calf Raise	3	20	30 seconds	#11
Marching in Place	3	90 secs	30 seconds	#38

Week Four – Workout #2

Exercise	Sets	Reps	Rest	Exercise Number
		Warm Up Session		
Wall Push-Ups	3	15-20	30 seconds	#31
Push-Ups	3	4-12	60 seconds	#34
Knee Push-Ups	3	10-15	45 seconds	#33
Tricep Dips	3	10-15	30 seconds	#43
Side Lying Leg Circles	3 (each leg)	15	30 seconds	#42
Reverse Abdominal Crunches	3	6-15	45 seconds	#46
Side Plank	3 (each side)	30 secs	30 seconds	#45

Week Four – Workout #3

Exercise	Sets	Reps	Rest	Exercise Number
		Warm Up Session		
Seated Hamstring Curls	3 (each leg)	15	30 seconds	#13
Single Leg Box Squat	3 (each leg)	5	45 seconds	#5
Squats while Holding Chair	3	15-20	30 seconds	#23
Bodyweight Squats	3	15-20	30 seconds	#35

Exercise	Sets	Reps	Rest	Exercise Number
		Warm Up Session		
Single-Leg Romanian Deadlifts	3 (each leg)	15	30 seconds	#25
Walking Lunges	4	20	60 seconds	#41
Lateral Lunges	3 (each leg)	15	30 seconds	#22

Week Four – Workout #4

Exercise	Sets	Reps	Rest	Exercise Number
		Warm Up Session		
Box Push-Ups	3	15-20	30 seconds	#32
Push-Ups	3	4-12	60 seconds	#34
Knee Push-Ups	3	10-15	45 seconds	#33
Seated Resistance Band Bicep Curl	3 (each arm)	15-20	30 seconds	#29
Seated Toe Taps	3	15-20	30-60 seconds	#30
Wood Chops	3 (each arm)	15	60-90 seconds	#47
Plank	3	30 secs	30 seconds	#44

Seniors with High Mobility – Workouts Week Five

(4 *workouts*)

Week Five – Workout #1

Exercise	**Sets**	**Reps**	**Rest**	**Exercise Number**
Warm Up Session				
Seated Hamstring Curls with Resistance Band	3 (each leg)	15	30 seconds	#14
Sumo Squats while Holding Chair	3	15-20	60 seconds	#24
Seated Leg Extension with Ankle Weights	3 (each leg)	15	30 seconds	#7
Lateral Lunges	3 (each leg)	15	30 seconds	#40
Glute Bridges	3	15-20	30 seconds	#39
Seated Calf Raise	3	20	30 seconds	#11
Marching in Place	3	90 secs	30 seconds	#38

Week Five – Workout #2

Exercise	**Sets**	**Reps**	**Rest**	**Exercise Number**
Warm Up Session				
Wall Push-Ups	3	15-20	30 seconds	#31
Push-Ups	3	4-12	60 seconds	#34
Knee Push-Ups	3	10-15	45 seconds	#33
Tricep Dips	3	10-15	30 seconds	#43
Side Lying Leg Circles	3 (each leg)	15	30 seconds	#42
Reverse Abdominal Crunches	3	6-15	45 seconds	#46
Side Plank	3 (each side)	30 secs	30 seconds	#45

Week Five – Workout #3

Exercise	**Sets**	**Reps**	**Rest**	**Exercise Number**
Warm Up Session				
Seated Hamstring Curls	3 (each leg)	15	30 seconds	#13
Single Leg Box Squat	3 (each leg)	5	45 seconds	#5
Squats while Holding Chair	3	15-20	30 seconds	#23
Bodyweight Squats	3	15-20	30 seconds	#35

Exercise	Sets	Reps	Rest	Exercise Number
Warm Up Session				
Single-Leg Romanian Deadlifts	3 (each leg)	15	30 seconds	#25
Walking Lunges	4	20	60 seconds	#41
Lateral Lunges	3 (each leg)	15	30 seconds	#22

Week Five – Workout #4

Exercise	Sets	Reps	Rest	Exercise Number
Warm Up Session				
Box Push Ups	3	15-20	30 seconds	#32
Push-Ups	3	4-12	60 seconds	#34
Knee Push-Ups	3	10-15	45 seconds	#33
Seated Resistance Band Bicep Curl	3 (each arm)	15-20	30 seconds	#29
Seated Toe Taps	3	15-20	30-60 seconds	#30
Wood Chops	3 (each arm)	15	60-90 seconds	#47
Plank	3	30 secs	30 seconds	#44

Seniors with High Mobility – Workouts Week Six

(4 *workouts*)

Week Six – Workout #1

Exercise	Sets	Reps	Rest	Exercise Number
Warm Up Session				
Seated Hamstring Curls with Resistance Band	3 (each leg)	20	30 seconds	#14
Sumo Squats while Holding Chair	3	20	60 seconds	#24
Seated Leg Extension with Ankle Weights	3 (each leg)	20	30 seconds	#7
Lateral Lunges	3 (each leg)	20	30 seconds	#40
Glute Bridges	3	20	30 seconds	#39
Seated Calf Raise	3	20	30 seconds	#11
Marching in Place	3	90 secs	30 seconds	#38

Week Six – Workout #2

Exercise	Sets	Reps	Rest	Exercise Number
Warm Up Session				
Wall Push-Ups	3	20	30 seconds	#31
Push-Ups	3	6-15	60 seconds	#34
Knee Push-Ups	3	20	45 seconds	#33
Tricep Dips	3	20	30 seconds	#43
Side Lying Leg Circles	3 (each leg)	20	30 seconds	#42
Reverse Abdominal Crunches	3	8-15	45 seconds	#46
Side Plank	3 (each side)	30 secs	30 seconds	#45

Week Six – Workout #3

Exercise	Sets	Reps	Rest	Exercise Number
Warm Up Session				
Seated Hamstring Curls	3 (each leg)	20	30 seconds	#13
Single Leg Box Squat	3 (each leg)	6-10	45 seconds	#5
Squats while Holding Chair	3	20	30 seconds	#23
Bodyweight Squats	3	20	30 seconds	#35

Exercise	Sets	Reps	Rest	Exercise Number
Warm Up Session				
Single-Leg Romanian Deadlifts	3 (each leg)	20	30 seconds	#25
Walking Lunges	4	20	60 seconds	#41
Lateral Lunges	3 (each leg)	20	30 seconds	#22

Week Six – Workout #4

Exercise	Sets	Reps	Rest	Exercise Number
Warm Up Session				
Box Push-Ups	3	20	30 seconds	#32
Push-Ups	3	6-15	60 seconds	#34
Knee Push-Ups	3	20	45 seconds	#33
Seated Resistance Band Bicep Curl	3 (each arm)	20	30 seconds	#29
Seated Toe Taps	3	20	30-60 seconds	#30
Wood Chops	3 (each arm)	20	60-90 seconds	#47
Plank	3	30 secs	30 seconds	#44

Seniors with High Mobility – Workouts Week Seven

(4 *workouts*)

Week Seven – Workout #1

Exercise	Sets	Reps	Rest	Exercise Number
Warm Up Session				
Seated Hamstring Curls with Resistance Band	3 (each leg)	20	30 seconds	#14
Sumo Squats while Holding Chair	3	20	60 seconds	#24
Seated Leg Extension with Ankle Weights	3 (each leg)	20	30 seconds	#7
Lateral Lunges	3 (each leg)	20	30 seconds	#40
Glute Bridges	3	20	30 seconds	#39
Seated Calf Raise	3	20	30 seconds	#11
Marching in Place	3	120 secs	30 seconds	#38

Week Seven – Workout #2

Exercise	Sets	Reps	Rest	Exercise Number
Warm Up Session				
Wall Push-Ups	3	20	30 seconds	#31
Push-Ups	3	8-15	60 seconds	#34
Knee Push-Ups	3	20	45 seconds	#33
Tricep Dips	3	20	30 seconds	#43
Side Lying Leg Circles	3 (each leg)	20	30 seconds	#42
Reverse Abdominal Crunches	3	10-20	45 seconds	#46
Side Plank	3 (each side)	40 secs	30 seconds	#45

Week Seven – Workout #3

Exercise	Sets	Reps	Rest	Exercise Number
Warm Up Session				
Seated Hamstring Curls	3 (each leg)	20	30 seconds	#13
Single Leg Box Squat	3 (each leg)	10-15	45 seconds	#5
Squats while Holding Chair	3	20	30 seconds	#23
Bodyweight Squats	3	20	30 seconds	#35

Exercise	Sets	Reps	Rest	Exercise Number
Warm Up Session				
Single-Leg Romanian Deadlifts	3 (each leg)	20	30 seconds	#25
Walking Lunges	4	20	60 seconds	#41
Lateral Lunges	3 (each leg)	20	30 seconds	#22

Week Seven – Workout #4

Exercise	Sets	Reps	Rest	Exercise Number
Warm Up Session				
Box Push-Ups	3	20	30 seconds	#32
Push-Ups	3	8-15	60 seconds	#34
Knee Push-Ups	3	20	45 seconds	#33
Seated Resistance Band Bicep Curl	3 (each arm)	20	30 seconds	#29
Seated Toe Taps	3	20	30-60 seconds	#30
Wood Chops	3 (each arm)	20	60-90 seconds	#47
Plank	3	40 secs	30 seconds	#44

Seniors with High Mobility – Workouts Week Eight

(4 *workouts*)

Week Eight – Workout #1

Exercise	Sets	Reps	Rest	Exercise Number
Warm Up Session				
Seated Hamstring Curls with Resistance Band	3 (each leg)	20	30 seconds	#14
Sumo Squats while Holding Chair	3	20	60 seconds	#24
Seated Leg Extension with Ankle Weights	3 (each leg)	20	30 seconds	#7
Lateral Lunges	3 (each leg)	20	30 seconds	#40
Glute Bridges	3	20	30 seconds	#39
Seated Calf Raise	3	20	30 seconds	#11
Marching in Place	3	120 secs	30 seconds	#38

Week Eight – Workout #2

Exercise	Sets	Reps	Rest	Exercise Number
		Warm Up Session		
Wall Push-Ups	3	20	30 seconds	#31
Push-Ups	3	10-15	60 seconds	#34
Knee Push-Ups	3	20	45 seconds	#33
Tricep Dips	3	20	30 seconds	#43
Side Lying Leg Circles	3 (each leg)	20	30 seconds	#42
Reverse Abdominal Crunches	3	12-20	45 seconds	#46
Side Plank	3 (each side)	40 secs	30 seconds	#45

Week Eight – Workout #3

Exercise	Sets	Reps	Rest	Exercise Number
		Warm Up Session		
Seated Hamstring Curls	3 (each leg)	20	30 seconds	#13
Single Leg Box Squat	3 (each leg)	12-20	45 seconds	#5
Squats while Holding Chair	3	20	30 seconds	#23
Bodyweight Squats	3	20	30 seconds	#35

Exercise	Sets	Reps	Rest	Exercise Number
Warm Up Session				
Single-Leg Romanian Deadlifts	3 (each leg)	20	30 seconds	#25
Walking Lunges	4	20	60 seconds	#41
Lateral Lunges	3 (each leg)	20	30 seconds	#22

Week Eight – Workout #4

Exercise	Sets	Reps	Rest	Exercise Number
Warm Up Session				
Box Push-Ups	3	20	30 seconds	#32
Push-Ups	3	10-15	60 seconds	#34
Knee Push-Ups	3	20	45 seconds	#33
Seated Resistance Band Bicep Curl	3 (each arm)	20	30 seconds	#29
Seated Toe Taps	3	20	30-60 seconds	#30
Wood Chops	3 (each arm)	20	60-90 seconds	#47
Plank	3	40 secs	30 seconds	#44

CHAPTER 11

Working Out Frequently Asked Questions

How Long Should My Workout Last?

Ideally, you want your workouts to last less than 60 minutes, but this only matters if you are training at a high intensity. It won't matter if your workout goes over this time for lower-intensity workouts. However, the workouts are designed to be much shorter than that.

Can I Rest for Longer than the Advised Time?

Absolutely. The rest periods are there as general guidance, but the important thing for you to do is to listen to your body. If you are breathing hard and feel fatigued, then rest for longer. If you feel fresh and want to start your next set quicker, then go for it.

For Single Arm or Leg Exercises, Do I Split the Rep Number in Half?

No. The rep number is for each arm. So if your exercise says "1 set (each arm) 20 reps", then you would perform 20 reps with your right arm, followed by 20 reps on your left arm. Rather than just performing ten reps each time.

I Can't Hit the Minimum Rep Number for an Exercise

That's fine! If you are one or two reps off, then do that. If you are supposed to be performing 20 reps and struggling to perform two reps, then the exercise may be too strenuous for you. Or you are too tired from the rest of the workout. For the next workout, swap the order so that you perform that exercise first. If you are still struggling, remove the exercise or go back a couple of weeks.

Should I See a Doctor Before I Begin?

This is an excellent idea. Particularly if you have an illness or take medication. But the workouts have been designed for seniors with differing abilities, so your doctor is unlikely to have any issue with you performing the program. Showing your workout plan to a physio beforehand might also be a good idea, particularly if you have any injuries.

What Time of Day Should I Train?

It doesn't matter. Just pick a time that suits your lifestyle. You want to choose a time when you are motivated to exercise. For some people, this will be first thing in the morning. For others, it may be last thing at night.

Should I Perform a Cool-Down?

Cool-downs can be an excellent way to lower your heart rate gently, but they aren't as valuable as warm-ups. If you want to perform a cool-down, a walk in the park after your workout is a great option.

My Muscles Hurt After My Workout. Is there a Problem?

Delayed-Onset Muscle Soreness (DOMS) is a common condition, particularly with new exercisers. For the first couple weeks of a new training program, you will almost certainly feel muscle pain for a day or two after each workout. That's why the low-mobility and medium-mobility eight-week programs have two weeks of limited training. To give you a chance to recover.

You can reduce DOMS by having a warm bath, walking (gentle exercise can help transport blood to the muscles), and sleeping well.

If you are feeling DOMS after every session and have been training for four weeks, this may indicate that your recovery isn't excellent. Try sleeping more, reducing your weekly training sessions, and giving yourself more rest between sets.

After Reading an Exercise Description, I am Still Unsure of How to Perform it.

This is understandable. Some exercises need to be seen! Each exercise in Balance Exercise For Seniors 50, 60 and Beyond is accompanied by a QR code, scan it with your mobile to watch a video clip of the exercise.

CHAPTER 12

Final Thoughts

'Take pride in how far you've come. Have faith in how far you can go. But don't forget to enjoy the journey'.

Michael Josephson

Congratulations! If you've made it this far, you are well on your way to improved balance, strength, and fitness. Take things slowly, listen to your body throughout, and ensure that the area where you are training is safe and contains no hazards.

Improving your balance is not just about strengthening your core muscles or learning complicated movements. It is also about building your confidence and awareness of your body. It can be frustrating at first, some exercises can take a long time to master, but *the juice is worth the squeeze.*

Once you have improved your balance, you will be able to live a more independent life, have more options open to you, and improve your health and fitness. So don't worry if your first or even thirtieth session was brutal. You will get there.

Good luck!

Spread the Word

If you enjoyed this book as much as I have enjoyed writing it, and if you feel (as I surely hope) that the balance exercises and workouts that you've received here will positively improve your lifestyle and allow you to live without the fear of falling, please tell others.

Spread the word by referrals to friends, family, and other seniors (and soon-to-be seniors) whom you know, and who you think can benefit.

Our Community:

To be one of the first people to receive notification of future books in the series "For Seniors 50, 60 and Beyond" when they are released join our community. I'll personally notify you as soon the next book in the series is available. Our monthly newsletter also contains tip, tricks and advice to help you on your fitness journey.

As a member you have access to the exercise videos directly from our website ***www.iaa.pub*,** without the need to scan individual QR codes within the book. Plus **Exclusive Members Access** to workout videos showing all the exercises contained in each of the workouts (not available from within the book via QR codes), a great reference and time saver!

Finally, I wish to thank you so much for reading Balance Exercise *for Seniors 50, 60 and Beyond*. It was written to provide helpful information to seniors wishing to improve their balance. I hope that you'll use what you have learnt to banishing the fear of falling and boost your self-confidence!

I Have A Favor To Ask:

Would you please take a couple of minutes to write a review of this book on Amazon? I'll be checking the reviews personally and your honest feedback will help me better help others on improve their balance and banish their fears.

To Leave A Review:

You can either:

- Scan the QR Code on your mobile

- Visit Amazon's website, search *Balance Exercise for Seniors 50, 60 and Beyond*. Click the link for this book, scroll down, and click on "Write a Customer Review."

Thank you very much, and I look forward to reading your comments!

David O'Connor

For Seniors 50, 60 and Beyond

BOOK SERIES

Book 1: **Fitness For Seniors 50, 60 and Beyond**

It's never too early to improve your fitness and definitely never to late to start. Consider this a fitness guide book, dip into to its sections as and when required.

Book 2: **Resistance Bands For Seniors 50, 60 and Beyond**

Strength and flexibility training without the need to purchase expensive weights and with less risk of injury, or a gym membership.

Book 3: **Balance Exercise For Seniors 50, 60 and Beyond**

Improve your balance to significantly reduce the risk and overcome the fear of falling. Live an active life in your golden years with increased self-confidence.

Book 4: **Chair Yoga For Seniors 50, 60 and Beyond**

All the benefits of yoga achievable while sitting or using a chair for additional support. Chair yoga offers variations that are perfect for seniors, even for those with limited mobility.

Book 5: **Stretches For Seniors 50, 60 and Beyond**

Stretches to improve flexibility, balance, mobility and reduce muscle pain for beginner through to advanced practitioners. Stretching helps release muscle tension, soreness and reduces the risk of injury.

Book 6: **Core Training For Seniors 50, 60 and Beyond**

A strong core stabilizes your entire body, providing better balance and posture. Core strength is essential at any age but especially as you get older and your risk of falling increases.

An overview of the For Seniors 50, 60 and Beyond book series is available at www.iaa.pub or scan the QR code.

SCAN FOR BOOK INFORMATION

Exercise Index

References

[1] Freiberger, E., Sieber, C. C., & Kob, R. (2020). Mobility in Older Community-Dwelling Persons: A Narrative Review. *Frontiers in Physiology*, 11. https://doi.org/10.3389/fphys.2020.00881

[2] *Physical Activity for Healthy Aging*. (2022, June 3). Centers for Disease Control and Prevention. https://www.cdc.gov/physicalactivity/basics/older_adults/index.htm

[3] Schoenborn, C. A., Adams, P. F., & Peregoy, J. A. (2013). Health behaviors of adults: United States, 2008–2010. *Vital and Health Statistics. Series 10, Data from the National Health Survey*, 10(257), 1–184. https://pubmed.ncbi.nlm.nih.gov/25116426/

[4] *Keep on Your Feet*. (2020, December 16). Centers for Disease Control and Prevention. https://www.cdc.gov/injury/features/older-adult-falls/index.html

[5] Busse, A. L., Gil, G., Santarém, J. M., & Jacob Filho, W. (2009). Physical activity and cognition in the elderly: A review. *Dementia & Neuropsychologia*, 3(3), 204–208. https://doi.org/10.1590/s1980-57642009dn30300005

[6] Harvard Health. (2021, February 15). *Exercise can boost your memory and thinking skills*. Retrieved

August 8, 2022, from https://www.health.harvard.edu/mind-and-mood/exercise-can-boost-your-memory-and-thinking-skills

[7] Harvard Health. (2019, May 1). *More evidence that exercise can boost mood.* Retrieved August 8, 2022, from https://www.health.harvard.edu/mind-and-mood/more-evidence-that-exercise-can-boost-mood

[8] Sharma, A., Madaan, V., & Petty, F. D. (2006). Exercise for Mental Health. *The Primary Care Companion to The Journal of Clinical Psychiatry*, 08(02), 106. https://doi.org/10.4088/pcc.v08n0208a

[9] Blundell, J. E., Gibbons, C., Caudwell, P., Finlayson, G., & Hopkins, M. (2015). Appetite control and energy balance: impact of exercise. *Obesity Reviews*, 16, 67–76. https://doi.org/10.1111/obr.12257

[10] Rob Newsom. (2022, March 18). *Aging and Sleep.* Sleep Foundation. Retrieved August 8, 2022, from https://www.sleepfoundation.org/aging-and-sleep

[11] Reid, K. J., Baron, K. G., Lu, B., Naylor, E., Wolfe, L., & Zee, P. C. (2010). Aerobic exercise improves self-reported sleep and quality of life in older adults with insomnia. *Sleep Medicine*, 11(9), 934–940. https://doi.org/10.1016/j.sleep.2010.04.014

[12] Rogers, M. E, Page, P., & Takeshima, N. (2013). Balance Training for the Older Athlete. *International Journal of Sports Physical Therapy*, 8(4), 517–530. https://www.ncbi.nlm.nih.gov/pmc/articles/PMC3812830/

[13] Borowicz, A., Zasadzka, E., Gaczkowska, A., Gawłowska, O., & Pawlaczyk, M. (2016). Assessing gait and balance impairment in elderly residents of nursing homes. *Journal of Physical Therapy Science*, 28(9), 2486–2490. https://doi.org/10.1589/jpts.28.2486

[14] El-Kashlan, H. K., Shepard, N. T., Asher, A. M., Smith-Wheelock, M., & Telian, S. A. (1998, March). Evaluation of Clinical Measures of Equilibrium. *The Laryngoscope*, 108(3), 311–319. https://doi.org/10.1097/00005537-199803000-00002

[15] Laukkanen, J, S Kurl, R Salonen, R Rauramaa, J Salonen (2004): The predictive value of cardiorespiratory fitness for cardiovascular events in men with various risk profiles: a prospective population-based cohort study, in: *European Heart Journal, Oxford University Press* (OUP), vol. 25, no. 16, pp. 1428–1437, [online] doi:10.1016/j.ehj.2004.06.013.

Printed in Great Britain
by Amazon

26570790R00192